NEW Backyard
IDEA BOOK

NATALIE ERMANN RUSSELL

NEW Backyard

IDEA BOOK

The Taunton Press

For Steve, Sam, and Baby Mel

The Taunton Press, Inc.

63 South Main Street

PO Box 5506

Newtown, CT 06470-5506

e-mail: tp@taunton.com

Editors: Erica Sanders-Foege, Heather Paper

Copy editor: Karen Fraley

Jacket/Cover design: Kimberly Adis

Interior design: Kimberly Adis

Layout: Laura Lind Design

Illustrator: Jean Tuttle, except for illustration on p. 175 by Ron Cascio, courtesy *Fine Homebuilding*, © The Taunton Press, Inc.

Cover Photographers: Front cover: (left, top to bottom) photo © Mark Lohman, Design: Rhino Sports/Dream Courts; photo © Jack Coyier, Design: ARTECHO Architecture and Landscape Architecture/Pamela Palmer, www.artecho.com; photo courtesy of Tumbleweed Houses, tumbleweedhouses.com; (middle) photo © Brian Vanden Brink; (right, top to bottom) photo © Jennifer Cheung and Steven Nilsson, Design: Heather Lenkin of www.lenkindesign.com; photo © Jack Coyier, Design: Katie Moss Landscape Design, www.katiemoss.com; photo © Mark Lohman, Design: Houston/Tyner Architects, Brad Jenson Construction, and Kathryne Designs; Back cover: (top left) photo © Mali Azima; (bottom left) photo © Smith and Hawken; (middle) photo (c) Jack Coyier, Design: John Bilac, Picture Perfect Construction (installation), www.pictureperfectconstruction.com; (right) photo © Eric Roth

Library of Congress Cataloging-in-Publication Data

Russell, Natalie.

New backyard idea book / Natalie Ermann Russell.

p. cm.

ISBN 978-1-60085-132-2

1. Backyard gardens--Design. 2. Garden structures--Design and construction. I. Title.

SB473.R93 2010

717--dc22

2009033535

Printed in the United States of America

10 9 8 7 6 5 4 3 2 1

The following names/manufacturers appearing in *New Backyard Idea Book* are trademarks: Astroturf®, Ping-Pong®

acknowledgments

JUST AS ASSEMBLING A PICTURE-PERFECT BACKYARD REQUIRES MANY HANDS, so, too, did putting together this book. Without the work of a talented team of editors, photographers, and designers, it would never have materialized.

A special thanks to photographers Jack Coyier and Mark Lohman, as well as Jennifer Cheung and Steven Nilsson, for their ability to capture the essence of such a wide variety of backyards. And to designers Heather Lenkin of Lenkin Design, Katie Moss of Katie Moss Landscape Design, Pamela Palmer of ARTECHO Architecture and Landscape Architecture, and Jon Goldstein of Jonny Appleseed Landscape Inc., thank you for sharing with us your vision, time,

and expertise. And, of course, a big note of gratitude goes to all of the homeowners who opened their backyards to our cameras, offering us a glimpse of some amazing landscapes.

I'd also like to thank Taunton senior editor Erica Sanders-Foege, editor Heather Paper, editorial assistant Catherine Levy, and photo editor Katy Binder for all of their guidance and support, as well as all of the other editors and designers, and the production team, who helped transform these words and photographs into a beautiful, practical book.

contents

introduction

FEW THINGS ARE MORE ALL-AMERICAN THAN THE BACKYARD. It brings to mind cherished memories in every season: picnics amid the vibrant blooms in spring, water games in summer, cocktails by a bonfire in fall, and building snowmen in winter.

This little patch of land wasn't always so revered. It was long associated with the outhouse. But once indoor plumbing took hold in the early 20th century, the backyard became the land of possibilities that it is today.

With minimal acreage, you can create a lush garden, a pool for exercise or play, even an outdoor kitchen, living area, or dining room. And backyard structures can run the gamut from gazebos and pool houses to private studios. The options are many, no matter what your budget may be.

Especially for complex backyard projects, a professional can be a vital resource and a worthwhile expense. A landscape designer or architect can help you come up with a plan for a relatively small fee, even if you don't immediately implement it entirely. You can find a pro in your area by visiting the Association of Professional Landscape Designers website (www.apld.com) or that of the American Society of Landscape Architects (www.asla.org).

Once you've narrowed your search to a few candidates, interview them to find one that best suits your vision—and your budget.

Once you have a professional on board, discuss in more depth how you see the yard taking shape in your mind's eye, and how you plan to use it. Will you entertain frequently? Would you like to hide an eyesore with pants? Are you interested in low-maintenance options?

With plan in hand, you can make the transformation happen in stages or wait until time and budget allow for contractors to do it all at once. Or if you're handy and have a green thumb, you can implement the plan yourself.

The goal is, of course, to have a backyard that lures you out into it every day—like the fabulous examples you'll see in this book. Dog-ear the pages; show them to your designer. Using these ideas as inspiration, you can have your own picture-perfect paradise just steps away from the back door.

porches, patios, and decks

• • •

THE BEST PART OF HAVING A PORCH, PATIO, OR DECK IS THAT IT'S A great excuse to spend more time outside, whether to cook, eat, play, read, or just relax. Porches are usually raised and have a roof and/or walls. Patios are typically open to the sky and are flush with the ground, but still have distinct flooring (stone, concrete, or even wood). Like a porch, a deck is almost always elevated, but it doesn't have a roof. It is particularly functional when you want to extend a room that is not on the ground floor—like a dining or living room in a house on a slope.

Deciding which type of outdoor living area is right for you depends on your climate and lifestyle. If you live in a region with mild winters, you may want something open and airy that can be used year-round. If you live in a woodsy area with lots of insects, you may opt for the protection a screened-in porch provides. If you frequently grill out, you may prefer a deck or patio, both of which—because they are open—don't require any ventilation.

Before getting too far into the process, check your local regulations, since some porches, patios, and decks can legally increase the square footage of your home, and therefore violate zoning bylaws (some of which restrict house-to-yard ratio). As always, a little research beforehand could save you money and anxiety in the end.

A narrow porch is deceptively airy thanks to a blue ceiling.

porches

● ● ● IDEALLY, A PORCH WILL INTERACT WITH THE REST OF your yard to bring the outdoors closer. In fact, it can act as a seamless link between the inside and outside, especially if you create more than one entry point. Two sets of French doors—placed side-by-side or a few feet apart—can be thrown wide open to let in fresh air and views, providing an alfresco experience even when you're not actually out on the porch.

Before there was television, front porches functioned as a spot for entertainment and socialization. Today, homeowners crave more privacy, and a backyard porch delivers: the serenity of outdoor living, without the intrusion of people and cars passing by.

To figure out the right size porch to build, buy the furniture you want beforehand and set it out in the yard where the structure will eventually be. Choose pieces in keeping with how you want to use the space: Quiet dinners for two? Entertaining large groups? A comfy spot for reading? This way you can experiment with an arrangement that suits your lifestyle and determine the right square footage for your needs—and for your furnishings. Also factor in the architecture of your home, so the porch is in keeping with both its style and size.

Even a narrow porch can accommodate comfortable seating, a point proven by these straightforward loveseats. A natural-wood ceiling and lush hanging plants add texture to the space while still keeping it simple.

Seating pieces covered in cool-colored
fabrics create a soothing area for relaxing
or entertaining in this outdoor living room.
The arched doorway and pillars add drama,
framing the view of the yard beyond.

On a porch that has all the features of a fine interior room, a fireplace and rustic brick wall add irresistible warmth, making the space appealingly cozy and romantic even on a chilly evening.

more about...
BLUE PORCH CEILINGS

ravel around the United States and you'll see many a beadboard porch ceiling that's painted a light blue. The shade can vary from pale, pale blue to greenish-blue to a purpley blue.

So what's the purpose of this long-held tradition? The answer isn't as clear as the color, but it definitely has Southern roots. In South Carolina, for instance, any shade of blue used on porch ceilings is referred to as "haint blue"

and is believed to bring good luck, warding off evil spirits (a Gullah superstition). One unverifiable theory is that it keeps bugs and bees away; the insects think they're in a wide-open space and won't nest, fooled by the blue "sky."

Whether or not you place stock in either of these explanations, color theory tells us that any shade of blue is cooling and calming, which is reason enough to bring it to your porch.

LEFT Even though this porch has no railings, the bed of roses and plants clambering up the pillars create a natural barrier, giving the outdoor dining area a sense of privacy.

BELOW The same personal style that you apply indoors can be translated to the outdoors, too. Finishing touches—like this rug, pillows, and throw in warm terra-cotta colors—are what make the porch homey.

ENCLOSED PORCHES

enclosing a porch has the distinct advantage of keeping out the bugs while letting in the fresh air and sounds of nature. When considering doing this, think about screening just the windows, or using half walls or entire walls of screen for more complete views and to allow in more light and air.

Porches with fully insulated windows and walls can be used during most seasons, serving as year-round retreats even in areas with extreme winters. If the windows are south facing, you'll get the benefit of passive-solar heat from the abundant sunlight, which can save you money on bills. Well-insulated windows can make a difference, too.

When determining to which room you will attach the porch, take into consideration that it can greatly reduce the amount of natural light allowed into the interior. Make sure it's a room with plenty of supplemental lighting, and perhaps one used more at night than during the day.

TOP A large table on a screened-in porch makes you feel like you're eating in the woods, but without all of the insects. With a view like this, simple furniture and porch design complement without competing.

BOTTOM Even with dark wood on the ceiling, floor, and walls, this screened-in porch remains light and airy, thanks to the minimally obstructed screening that keeps views unimpeded.

ABOVE AND RIGHT Reminiscent of a luxury hotel in the tropics, this porch can be cordoned off with weather-resistant curtains. A sleeping spot, teamed here with a lamp made specifically for outdoor use, is an indulgent way to take advantage of a mild clime.

LEFT A floor painted in a jaunty checkerboard pattern gives a once-mundane porch a happy makeover. Even in partially protected spaces like this, it's important to use paints specifically formulated for outdoor porches and decks.

patios and terraces

●●● EVEN WITH A SMALL PATIO, YOU CAN HAVE A stellar outdoor retreat. A patio or terrace can be an extension of the house, so that as soon as you step outside, you've arrived. Or you can set it a few feet away. When detached, it becomes a separate destination.

The shape can also add to its personality. Neatly laid with square concrete pavers, it can have all the formality of a traditional home and garden. Or it can be an amorphous collection of flagstone, taking on the look of a natural clearing in the landscape.

If you choose to add a patio yourself, be sure to do research or consult a landscape design professional beforehand: You'll need the right amount of slope to ensure proper water drainage.

ABOVE A flagstone patio is encircled by the garden, climbing plants, and rounded boulders that soften the hard edges. The red Adirondack chairs add a vibrant pop and make it an appealing place for a casual gathering.

RIGHT This patio—simpatico with the architecture of the home in terms of color, material, and design—uses minimal furnishings to create maximum impact. A dining area and nearby chaise impart pure luxury.

FACING PAGE All it takes to warm up a concrete urban terrace are a few container plantings. This trio of purple flowering plants, teamed with a small Buddha statue, creates a feeling of serenity.

With just a little forethought, any space can feel like an indulgent retreat. Here, bright white cushions and vibrant accents—plus a delicate chandelier—turn what would otherwise have been a drab corner into an appealing hotspot.

RIGHT This slope provides a unique landscaping opportunity. The patio wall, its varied shades of gray tying in with the borders on the floor, visually blends with the nearby steps and rocks on the hillside.

BELOW Landscaped to establish it as a separate space from the house, this patio is still close enough to be convenient—the two linked with a multilevel deck. The combined outdoor living area is great for entertaining, as people can congregate in the various spots.

ABOVE A patio that serves as both an outdoor living room and kitchen makes entertaining enjoyable for the guests and easy for the host, thanks to the proximity of these areas to each other and the house.

RIGHT An open roof clearly defines an outdoor living area and still lets you enjoy a starry evening. Here, French doors unite inside and out—especially at dusk, when the indoor ambience spills onto the patio.

RIGHT A plastered-concrete half wall is a brilliant use of space; it can be for seating or displaying container plantings. Here, Arizona pink flagstone and terra-cotta–colored tile tie everything together visually.

ABOVE This patio-like space, set a distance away from the house, has a simplistic beauty. The rough stone steps and textured plantings leading to it—along with the fire pit—make the rustic nook an inviting destination.

RIGHT The entry into this space is framed by dramatically uplit bamboo clusters. The large copper pot to the left is just as functional as it is aesthetically pleasing; it can be filled with ice and beverages during parties.

• materials

The options for patio and terrace materials are virtually limitless in terms of color and shape, but pay attention to context when making your selection. A traditional home might look best with a brick patio, while a cottage might be best complemented by a freeform flagstone patio with moss in the joints.

You will want to consider a few practical factors as well. If you plan to have a dining table, for instance, a foundation made of loose pea gravel isn't ideal, because it can cause the table to wobble or even sink into the ground.

The materials you choose can also affect drainage. Products that are porous or pervious can be made to look just like concrete, brick, or stone, but allow water to penetrate and trickle down into the soil underneath. This is good for your peace of mind (no fear of flooding) and for the health of the environment, as it keeps water out of storm drains, reducing erosion and pollution.

A combination of materials can be attractive and practical, too. A concrete patio, for example, can be dressed up with a brick border that also serves to indicate grade changes or steps.

LEFT This approach to mixing materials utilizes fewer pavers—and more green grass—the farther you are from the house. The resulting pattern looks like a puzzle with so many pieces missing, creating a floor surface that's also a stunning decorative feature.

BELOW A random pattern of irregularly shaped stones pairs well with a timeworn metal table and chairs. The vegetation between the stones also softens the visual impression, contributing to the sense of elegant rusticity.

FACING PAGE In this alfresco eating area, a decomposed granite floor establishes a comfortable informality. Nearby, a partial concrete wall simultaneously creates a sense of privacy while functioning as a focal point, thanks to the uncomplicated wrought-iron artwork.

ABOVE The materials used here repeat throughout the property, making them a harbinger of everything you'll encounter outside this home. The blue "keystone" in the corner is lapis lazuli that was sourced from nearby mountains and points toward the pool.

LEFT Large slabs of granite used for this patio floor make for a sleek, modern aesthetic. The simplicity of this outdoor living area and the yard beyond keep it visually uncluttered, which suits a contemporary home.

FACING PAGE A patterned tile is sometimes too much for an entire patio space, but by employing it in different parts of the patio, separated by swaths of a more neutral material, it remains a highlight without becoming overwhelming.

RIGHT Reminiscent of a Mediterranean paradise, this patio's basket-weave–patterned terra-cotta tiles pair flawlessly with the furniture's fabric—as well as with the house itself—while small decorative tiles around the perimeter add further visual interest.

ABOVE This patio features an understated but intriguing palette of patterns and materials. The curvaceous silhouette of the chair is a welcome contrast to its more linear surrounds. Meanwhile, the built-in wood bench softens the primarily concrete space with its more organic personality.

LEFT Sizable concrete slabs divided by rivers of pebbles create a look that's both contemporary and casual. It also requires little more maintenance than periodically sweeping away any small stones that have become displaced.

RIGHT Contrasting floor materials are one of the best ways to define specific spaces. This patio's bar area is underscored with flagstone, while concrete is used for the general walkway.

A colorful tapestry of floor tiles suggests a Moroccan rug, without the maintenance. Choosing the same color palette for indoor and outdoor living rooms means you can pull favorite pieces outside (on a day without rain) and everything still blends beautifully.

gallery

small spaces

A sliver of a spot just outside a door or in a transitional area oftentimes is overlooked. If you have such a space, it might just need a comfortable chair and a side table to exploit its diminutive size. Small often equals cozy and personal, making a little nook feel like a very special place to hang out.

RIGHT A pair of unpretentious wooden folding chairs provide an inviting sitting spot just inside the fenceline of this residence, requiring no more than a sliver of space. The lightweight chairs are easy to pick up and move, too, when inclement weather is in the forecast.

BELOW Even a patio can stimulate all of the senses. The small water fountain provides a soothing trickle if someone should stop to rest on the stone bench. Moreover, the water feature, walkway, and bench echo the strong lines of the home's windows and doors, establishing design continuity.

ABOVE A hammock like this is the epitome of outdoor R&R but, when it's removed, the sandy floor beneath it doubles as a court for a European ball game.

LEFT This walkway is just wide enough to accommodate a comfortable chair and side table—and still let you pass by. Situated to provide a view of the yard, the sitting area offers a shady spot for relaxing.

decks

● ● ● THE TRADITIONAL WOOD DECK HAS GREAT APPEAL. IT'S a naturalistic perch from which you can take in the views. But not all wood is created equal.

Wood with large amounts of water (more than 30 percent) can shrink and warp, and is susceptible to rot and insects. "Dry" wood is better because it splits less frequently and is lighter. Wood that has been kiln dried is more expensive, but you can dry out wet wood yourself by stacking spacers between each piece and storing them in a dry area. (To determine the level of moisture in the wood you're considering, ask a salesperson to measure it with a moisture meter.)

If the health of the environment is a concern for you, opt for wood that is certified by the Forest Stewardship Council (FSC), which means the lumber has been harvested in an eco-friendly manner. Go to www.certifiedwood.org to find these certified products.

Finally, no matter what type of wood you use, be sure that it's properly installed by choosing a reputable contractor. If it's not, the boards can "cup," or warp into a curve.

LEFT A low-profile stone deck doesn't obscure the seemingly endless horizon surrounding this waterside home. Still, it has visual appeal of its own; the smooth floor pavers are a welcome contrast to the rough-hewn edges of the wall.

FACING PAGE The warm wood of this floor is echoed in the deck's railing, posts, and beams, which together create a rustic frame of the water view. Nothing more than a pair of chairs is needed here, providing an ideal spot for quiet contemplation.

A wood deck subtly links this house with a
cluster of trees in the backyard. Because it's
low to the ground, there's more of a one-with-
nature feeling.

more about...
WOOD TYPES

When planning a deck project, consider how your wood of choice will age in your climate. Will it turn a silvery gray or maintain a rich shade of brown? In addition to pure aesthetics, give some thought to price and upkeep, too.

1. Pressure-treated southern pine. If you opt for this type of wood, ask about and research the chemicals used. Although chromated copper arsenate (CCA), which contains arsenic, has been outlawed, any existing stock can still legally be sold. And even when treated, it requires maintenance that includes staining, sanding, and power-washing. Plus, it can have an unattractive greenish hue.

2. Cedar and redwood. These types of woods resist decay and pests, but require sealing and cleaning. They can be pricey but the look is gorgeous.

3. Tropical hardwoods. This category includes woods like ipe and massaranduba, which don't have to be chemically treated in order to resist decay but do have to be cleaned and oiled. Because these woods are very dense, they are extremely durable and shrink very little.

LEFT The clean lines of the slate tile deck are mimicked by the spiffy furniture and railings. The colorful potted plants and umbrellas add some curves to the mix, providing a refreshing balance.

ALTERNATIVES TO WOOD DECKING

because wood decks require regular maintenance, many companies have developed plastic lumber and wood-composite materials that mimic the appearance of wood but need less upkeep. Also, these low-maintenance options don't need to be stained or sealed, and don't become as weathered-looking as real wood. Plus, they tend to be insect-resistant, although the composite products are susceptible to mold and mildew. Due to a tendency to fade, composite decking is typically limited to light to medium colors. It stains easily, so any spills should be cleaned up right away.

Much of today's plastic lumber, another option, is made from recycled items such as milk jugs, grocery bags, and dry cleaning bags. The upside of this material is that it never has to be painted, and it won't stain or fade. It's also strong enough to be used for structural elements such as joists or girders, something that can't be said about composites. The downside is the price, which is typically higher than both wood and composite decking. But because it requires little maintenance, it can pay for itself over the long run.

LEFT Topping a porch with a second-floor deck maximizes your outdoor living space. This one feels particularly integral, thanks to lush plantings that link the two spaces.

FACING PAGE Building a deck right up to an existing tree creates a natural canopy for the space. The minimal ipe wood-and-wire cable railing also allows a nearly unobstructed view from the deck to the garden.

LEFT The color choice for the exterior of this house and deck make it look like the latter is an extension of the former. Unobstructive railings and a number of potted plants also connect it with the verdant backyard.

gallery

railings

Putting up railings is a safety consideration that doesn't have to take away from the beauty of your space. Railing materials run the gamut from vinyl to composites to wood to aluminum to wire. Styles are also quite diverse, so choose something in keeping with the architecture of your home.

BELOW For a more traditional deck, a wrought-iron railing is set off by the beautiful vista beyond. The curlicues even add interest to the flooring, as the high sun of midday casts a decorative shadow.

Wire cable and wood.

Contemporary wood and metal.

Sturdy ipe wood.

New Orleans–style metalwork.

Horizontal slats.

courtyards

●●● THE COURTYARD HAS A SPECIAL PLACE IN the American psyche. It conjures romantic visions of the Old World where courtyards are ubiquitous, and creates a private getaway. Of course, one great advantage of a courtyard is that you don't need a large space. In fact, a well-designed courtyard can add dimension to a narrow property by extending the sightlines and can provide that seclusion, even when your neighbors are just a few feet away.

A courtyard is typically surrounded by walls, but well-placed plants or trellises can generate a similar effect. If you have real walls, they can help improve safety and often provide enough protection to make you feel comfortable leaving the windows open.

A grassy courtyard bordered by the house itself can provide a sense of enclosure and feel spacious, too. This one features various shrub-lined gardens and a water feature in the center that functions as a focal point around which everything else revolves.

LEFT A brick-walled courtyard and the shelter of a tree together offer privacy from the neighbors. Creeping ivy, as well as container plantings throughout the courtyard, soften the look of the surrounding walls and the herringbone-patterned brick floor.

RIGHT The inherent hard surface of exterior walls can be softened with espaliered plants. Against this white wall, the curvaceous forms lend a timeworn elegance while making the nearby dining area feel cozier, too.

more about...
COURTYARD LAYOUT

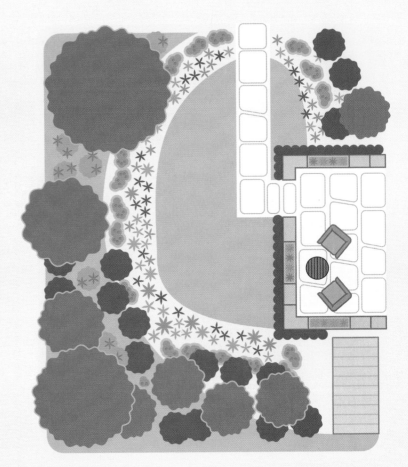

@ courtyard, which by definition is mostly or completely enclosed, becomes a hidden treasure in a backyard. The most important consideration is determining the dimensions of the space you want to create. Think about a small bedroom; that's the ideal size for a courtyard if you want to impart a sense of intimacy. To make it even more cozy, group seating pieces close enough to one another to facilitate conversation. When seated, people should be less than six feet apart.

Also consider how people will move through the space. Because a courtyard typically has walls, it's a destination rather than a pass-through. Give some thought to where they will be coming from—and where they will be moving to—by sketching the space on a piece of graph paper. If, for example, you have a doorway on the top left and another on the bottom right, mark both. Plot out the traffic pattern between the two, to indicate the "lane" that should not be obstructed by furnishings or other objects.

LEFT This brick-lined courtyard is an attractive pass-through, easing the transition between house and yard. It also steps in, as needed, as a gathering spot for large groups.

FACING PAGE The sturdy walls of this courtyard provide an ideal backdrop for an outdoor kitchen, with the appliances efficiently lined up in a row. Here, a vintage table provides a casual eating area but functions as an island, too.

LEFT A tiered fountain is the natural focus of this courtyard space, but the various textures surrounding it—from the flagstone floor to the river-rock wall to the brick border encircling the fountain itself—are just as visually appealing.

build a bamboo trellis

Courtyards don't have to be bordered by solid walls. A bamboo trellis entwined with climbing vines can have the same enclosed effect. Here's how to make one for your backyard.

SUPPLIES YOU WILL NEED
- Paper
- Pencil
- Hand saw
- Several canes of bamboo in different diameters
- Ruler or tape measure
- Lashing cord

❶ CREATE A DESIGN Imagine your trellis where it will eventually be placed, taking into account the size and shape of the area where it will be situated. Draw the design of your trellis on paper. Deciding on as many measurements as possible in advance will help you to stay on track during the building process.

❷ CUT THE BAMBOO TO SIZE Use a hand saw to cut the sky-facing ends of your vertical canes just above a node, which is solid. This will keep water from collecting in the open ends, which would encourage rot. Then cut the trimmed canes to size from the bottom. Cut the horizontal canes to size as well.

❸ LAY OUT YOUR TRELLIS On a flat surface, arrange the canes into the shape of your design, using a ruler to ensure that the canes are spaced evenly. Mark the intersecting points of the crossing canes with a pencil, since the unbound canes will shift around a bit as you start to connect them with lashing cord.

❹ LASH THEM TOGETHER Lash the crossing canes together as tightly as possible. Lashing is the most important part of making bamboo trellises, since it's what holds them together. Start with a piece of cord that's 4 to 5 feet long and trim the excess when you're done.

This project originally appeared in Fine Gardening, *No. 91*

Propping a bamboo trellis against a courtyard wall imparts a bit of nature and breaks up a boring expanse.

THE POSSIBILITIES ARE ENDLESS

Here is a selection of designs to give you a creative jump-start. Even subtle changes in sizing and spacing can give your bamboo trellis a distinctive look.

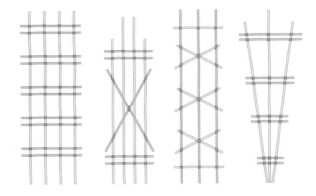

LASHING A TRELLIS

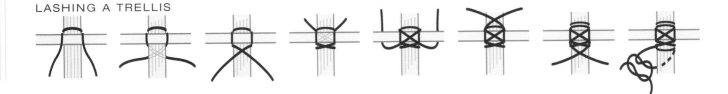

A view of a courtyard from a side portico can be quite captivating and romantic. If this is the case, be sure to consider how the courtyard plantings will look from that vantage point.

backyard entertaining

• • •

HAVING FRIENDS AND NEIGHBORS OVER FOR A BACKYARD BARBECUE is one of life's great pleasures. Amid the calming influence of nature, an outdoor affair seems less hectic than an indoor party. And who doesn't love grilled foods served with a side of fresh air? The experience can be improved not only with the right equipment and furnishings, but with the right attitude and finishing touches—the result being an entirely new outdoor room.

The style of your outdoor kitchen, living, or dining space will be greatly influenced by the architecture of your home and the natural elements of your backyard. You'll want good sunlight, but not so much that it becomes unbearably hot (in which case an awning or pergola can provide relief). You'll want a great view, without the intrusion of neighbors (hedges or other plantings that act as a screen can help here). And you'll want a spot with a pleasant breeze.

Your outdoor space should encourage mingling and draw people out into the yard. This can be achieved with paths, plantings, and garden ornaments. And a well-placed focal point—a fireplace, outdoor bar, garden fountain, or sculpture—is usually all it takes to lure someone farther away from the house, making your outdoor room seem even bigger.

A small patio like this is made even more inviting by an umbrella that cloaks the table and chairs from above, simulating a ceiling and making the space feel more like a room.

the basics

●●● THE WAY YOU SET UP YOUR OUTDOOR SPACE CAN shape how it will be used. Someone who entertains large groups will have different needs than someone who prefers intimate gatherings. If you do both, you'll need to create a plan for that as well.

To prepare food for a massive crowd, you'll want an outdoor kitchen with ample counter space and sufficient equipment. For dining, come up with a seating plan to supplement furniture groupings already in place. Reserve a grassy area for rental tables, or direct guests to perch-like walls and ledges, where they can mingle and chat while they graze. There doesn't have to be formal seating for everyone.

You may think that the larger the space is, the better it is for a big crowd, but that's not always true. Keeping people close engenders socializing and makes for better parties. And if your yard isn't very big, it actually will feel larger if you put up hedges or dividers to establish discrete "rooms" (a garden room and an outdoor dining room, for instance). When people are able to move from one distinct area to another, they are tricked into thinking there's more space than there really is.

ABOVE With all of the same luxuries as its indoor counterpart, this outdoor kitchen is a fun place for guests to congregate, thanks in part to comfortable bar stools and a TV suspended from the ceiling in the far corner.

RIGHT This space is appealing for the sole purpose of chilling out by the fire. And with a built-in grill adjacent to the fireplace, the host can prepare a meal without having to leave the party.

The pure simplicity of this breezy space allows it to embody quiet sophistication. The prevalent wood tones are softened with a paper lantern and free-flowing curtains, with just enough greenery thrown in to connect it with outdoors.

CONNECTING INDOORS AND OUT

One of the major goals of outdoor living is to link the inside to the outside discreetly, creating an open plan for unrestricted circulation. There are many ways to achieve this, including by attempting to bring the outdoors inside. This means installing an abundance of transparent materials, like glass or screen, to make the views of the yard part of the indoor scenery, almost like "living" wall art.

Another approach is to bring the indoors *out*. For example, carry the same flooring material from, say, the living room onto the porch, thus keeping the spaces visually united. You can take it even further by continuing all of the other decor choices outside too: Similar colors, fabrics, materials, and furniture styles. That way, there's a smooth shift from one to the other, and people will feel comfortable moving freely between them.

FACING PAGE
Simple caned stools are a good choice for a kids' table; they're inexpensive and lightweight. Positioning it beyond the living room's glass doors means parents can stay within earshot yet out of the way.

RIGHT This pass-through window folds back completely—a brilliant serving solution, especially when there's no outdoor kitchen. The stainless-steel countertop also functions as a walk-up-to bar where people can congregate.

ABOVE Sliding glass doors make the transition from indoor dining room to outdoor living room seamless. At a dinner party, guests can move organically from one to the other: appetizers outside, the main entrée inside, and back outside for dessert.

RIGHT The most effective transition is one that barely exists. These glass walls are actually sliding doors that glide to the side, immediately transporting you into the backyard landscape.

ABOVE Strategically placed umbrellas visually define this deck's kitchen, living, and dining areas. The warm color of the umbrellas—like the seat cushions—make the area even more inviting.

RIGHT The stone stools by this fire pit are a whimsical interpretation of wild mushrooms growing in the nearby forest. Just beyond, a pair of Adirondack chairs pull up to a table for dining alfresco.

more about ...
KITCHEN LAYOUTS

ONE LONG COUNTER

The components here are positioned one following the next. This layout works well against the back of the house (for easy access to utilities) and makes efficient use of a small space. If you have several types of appliances, place them in order of use: refrigerator, sink, grill, then a counter for serving.

TWO PARALLEL COUNTERS

An island without appliances, positioned to face the zone of greatest activity, becomes a vital extra workspace. The added square footage of countertop is indispensable for food prep. Or use it for dining by lining up bar stools on the opposite side.

L-SHAPED COUNTER

The L shape is effective when there are two cooks in the kitchen; by putting the grill on one side and the sink and refrigerator on the other, you can establish separate workstations. Keep in mind that each side needs at least three contiguous feet of counterspace to be functional.

U-SHAPED COUNTER

Ideal for large spaces, a U shape offers plenty of countertop and storage space. This one has three different work zones, which allows more than one person to be in the space at a time.

SQUARE COUNTER

A square layout is enclosed, except for a passageway in and out. It's best suited for one person, but because there are more useable sides, there is more room for appliances such as a brick oven and cooktop.

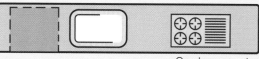
One long counter

Two parallel counters

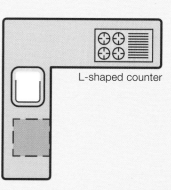
L-shaped counter

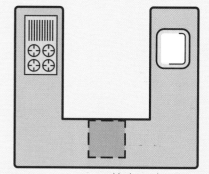
U-shaped counter

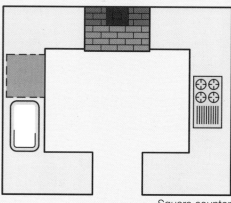
Square counter

more about ...
DINING AREAS

When shopping for dining furniture, first consider the size of your space and how you'll use it. A table that is 26 inches in diameter, like a bistro table, will seat two; a 48-inch round table will seat four to six, and a rectangular 72-inch by 36-inch table will seat eight.

But you'll need to account for more than the table itself; also plan for three feet of space behind each chair, so it can be pulled out without hindrance. Finally, if there are steps leading up to the dining area, leave five feet of open space between the table and the steps for safety.

ROOM TO DINE COMFORTABLY

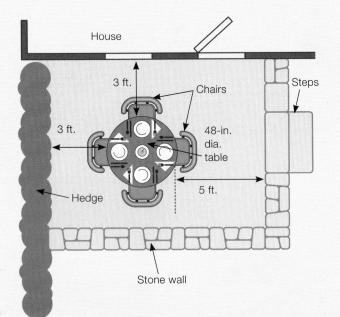

House

3 ft.

Chairs

Steps

3 ft.

48-in. dia. table

5 ft.

Hedge

Stone wall

Furnishings can be basic when another component has a bold personality. Here, the extrovert is the cobalt blue tile, which is outstanding against the pristine white of the house and the gleam of the stainless appliances.

When a grill is in an enclosed space like this, a ventilation hood is necessary to redirect the smoke. Here, the hood gets a customized makeover with a European design and a bit of "bon appetit."

This pillared porch becomes a transitional space between indoors and out, drawing guests toward a fully appointed living area on the adjacent patio. The conversation area is clearly defined by an easy-to-maintain outdoor rug.

ABOVE AND RIGHT Protected from the sun and summer showers by a retractable awning, this dining space has supplemental seating in the form of built-in benches. Because they are extra deep—a full three feet—guests can sprawl out and really get comfortable.

ARRANGING FURNITURE BY THE FIREPLACE

each outdoor room comes with its own set of challenges, so no single equation will solve every problem. But there are some basic guidelines to follow for furniture arrangement.

If your outdoor room has a fireplace, it's undoubtedly the focal point of the area, and therefore the main conversation group should be oriented toward the flames so that people can take pleasure in the view. Make sure there is enough space between the seating and the fireplace itself—at least eight feet—so you can feel the warmth but not obstruct a pathway. The seating pieces should be no more than six feet apart from one another, however, so that people can talk comfortably.

If the main component of your seating group is a pair of sofas, arrange the two facing each other in front of the fireplace. A single sofa, on the other hand, might face the fireplace, with its back to the entrance (steps, in this case) and flanked by chairs. If you choose the latter, make sure the sofa is just as attractive from the back as it is from the front, since that's the first thing you'll see when you ascend the steps. In fact, in many an outdoor room, furniture is seen from different vantage points, so make sure it is attractive from all angles.

Incorporating a built-in seating wall into a fireplace—and along the perimeter of the "room," for that matter—will add more sitting space, accommodating large groups when you entertain. But it will still look great when not in use, at which time you can turn it into a ledge for plants or sculpture.

Make the seat wall deeper than usual (24 inches or greater), so people can really stretch out and get comfortable, even lie down. And set the wall low (16 to 18 inches high) so that people sitting on the floor, on the wall, or on the chairs can all converse without feeling like they're at different levels. Also put out some floor pillows for a movable conversation hub.

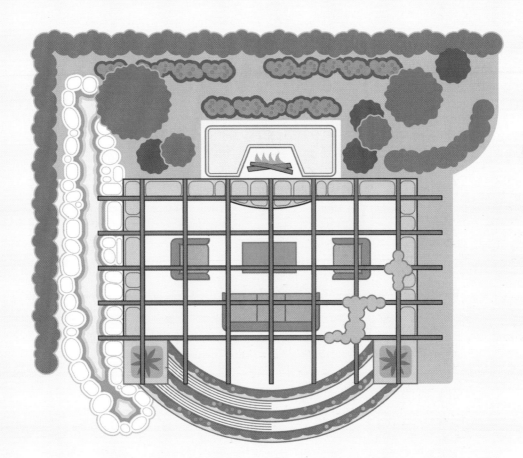

RIGHT The placement of appliances should be as efficient as possible. In this outdoor kitchen, the cooktop is positioned next to the grill, making you well-situated to keep an eye on both at the same time.

ABOVE When there's not enough overhead lighting—often the case in outdoor spaces—a counter-mounted lamp can be a great solution. This adjustable model can be focused directly on the grill or turned to illuminate the countertop.

•grills and appliances

How you equip your outdoor kitchen can greatly affect your enjoyment of preparing an outdoor meal. And when the work is more pleasurable, so, too, is eating the food.

There are gas grills, charcoal grills, hybrid grills (which operate on either or both gas and charcoal), wood-fired grills, and electric grills. Gas grills are most popular for their ease of use. They're quick starting and relatively eco-friendly, producing fewer carbon emissions than charcoal. Still, the gas-versus-charcoal battle wages on, as many purists believe the flavor imparted by charcoal is unparalleled. Hybrids offer the best of both, as they are easy to light but also infuse food with a lovely smokiness.

Grills are often sold by companies touting their BTUs (British thermal units), but more isn't necessarily better; a higher number of BTUs can mean more gas is consumed. Plus, there's only so much heat you need to cook a burger. The best approach is to research other features and the reliability of a particular product; don't make your choice based on BTUs alone.

Other outdoor appliances can cater to every need—or can be a little more simplistic. For example, you could install a bar caddy that chills with just ice or you could put in a refrigerator that would require an electrical hookup. What you select depends on your needs, habits, and of course, budget.

It's important to have a spot for your food before and after it's cooked. Having ample counter space on either side of the grill—at least 18 inches—makes preparation that much easier.

g a l l e r y

storage

Outdoor cabinetry has to be more durable than its indoor counterpart; it must withstand the weather conditions of your area and protect what's inside.

Wood. This material is most successful in dry climates, where it's less likely to mildew or warp. Even so, you want to use only rot-resistant types, like teak, ipe, or cedar. For extra protection, make sure wood cabinets are treated with stain, paint, or sealant.

Plastic. It may be called polymer, HDPE, or high-density polyethylene, but it all means plastic. This material has a very modern aesthetic, and won't rot, fade, or rust. (The very same substance is used on boats, so you know it's super sturdy.) To clean it, simply spray with a hose or wipe with a damp cloth.

Stainless steel. Because it matches many appliances, stainless steel is a popular choice. But all stainless steel isn't created equal. Pick a grade that is weather durable because lesser-quality steel is more likely to rust. And, for extra durability, make sure all of the components (even the hinges) are made of stainless.

1 Wood cabinets built in just below the grill provide easy access to serving dishes, bowls, and the like, while making good use of potentially wasted space.

2 A square kitchen design keeps all of these appliances in close proximity to one another. And there's ample stainless storage built into the concrete counters, one of the most durable surfaces you'll find.

3 Even a kitchen with an Old World feel can get away with modern stainless steel, thanks to a mix of other materials, including a concrete countertop, stone walls and veneer, and a paver floor.

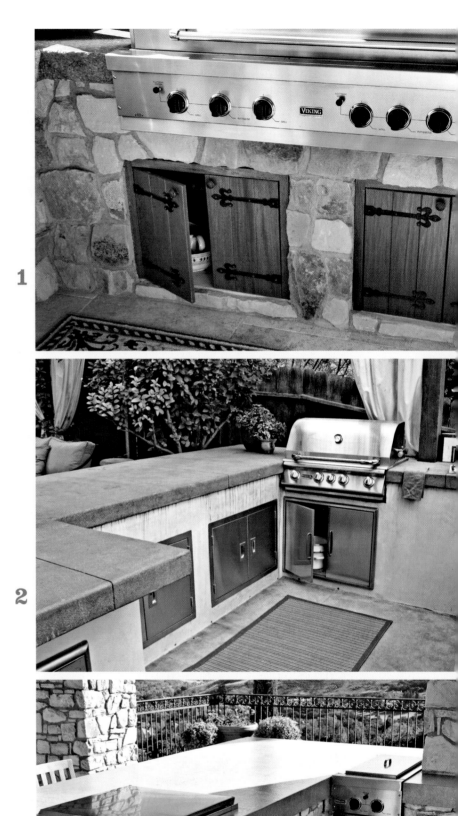

1

2

3

Made of concrete and simply powered by burning logs, this grill has a handy recess underneath to keep a sufficient stash of wood conveniently nearby.

FACING PAGE An outdoor refrigerator can be a lifesaver on a hot day, keeping beverages and fruit perfectly chilled. Look for a model with an automatic light, so you can see the contents even at night.

ABOVE An overhead heater can warm up to about 25 feet away, so tucking it out of sight ensures everyone is bathed in the warmth, and precious floor space is saved.

LEFT If you entertain frequently, a keg tap built into the counter can be ideal. Some models accommodate a full-size keg and others just a pony keg. You can even install one with two or three taps to give guests a selection.

ABOVE Even though it's an indulgence, an outdoor wood-fired pizza oven should be functional. Ample counterspace in front provides extra room for resting pizza peels and other equipment.

RIGHT This sink features an interior rim that accommodates a cutting board perfectly. Some of its other extras include, at the front, a stainless box that holds sponges and a metal dishtowel ring.

ABOVE AND LEFT This sink is like the type you'd find indoors, extra wide for washing dishes. The other is smaller, with a gooseneck faucet that is great for filling a tall flower vase with water.

• countertops and backsplashes

Even though the appearance of a countertop can set the tone for an entire outdoor kitchen, it is first and foremost a practical element. Tile, for example, comes in rich and vibrant colors, but has to be able to withstand freeze-and-thaw cycles without cracking in order to fare well in colder climates. Granite has an appealing textured look but, since it tends to retain heat, shouldn't be used in kitchens exposed to a lot of sunlight.

Concrete countertops—which can be stained, stamped, and embellished to emulate a wide variety of styles—are very durable but need to be resealed every so often. Flagstone is another beautiful option, but it can stain easily.

When selecting an outdoor countertop, you should consider what level of exposure to the natural elements it will have to endure and your appetite for maintenance. Only then can you can make a well-informed choice.

This one-of-a-kind bar was crafted using a treasured antique piece. Once a stone balcony in India, the architectural element now serves as a highly decorative front to this outdoor serving area.

Decorative tile can add pops of color to a countertop, giving it more visual interest. Here, a rectangle of artistic tiles breaks up the sea of solid color, taking on the look of a trivet.

Veneers, often used to cover the bases of islands or bars, are purely decorative, concealing the utility-grade, concrete-block structure beneath. The choices can be dizzying, but here are some of the most popular options:

Manufactured stone. It's usually a combination of cement and lightweight aggregate, but this material looks just like real stone. Due to its weight, shipping costs are lower and it doesn't stain or fade. But make sure you get pieces that are as natural-looking as you can because, when seen as a whole, the "stones'" fabricated look is a lot more obvious.

Natural stone. This choice looks more authentic than manufactured options, but cutting pieces to fit can be challenging—and expensive. With natural stone, choose material from local quarries to reduce cost and pollution created by shipping long distances.

Brick. If your home is made of brick, then having a brick grill island creates continuity in your backyard setting. You can have brick installed using spacers, so they're exactly straight, or allow some "sway," or imperfection, in the stacking for a more rustic, aged look.

Stucco. Durable and subtle, stucco does require some maintenance. It should be cleaned and painted from time to time, as it has a tendency to become soiled or chipped.

LEFT A green stone countertop is a real eye-catcher, especially set against the stacked-stone base. It's a durable surface on which to prepare food, and is aesthetically pleasing for diners, too.

RIGHT A concrete countertop is durable and withstands heat well, but needs to be resealed occasionally. Look for a product made with recycled concrete or fly ash, both of which make it more earth-friendly.

ABOVE Throughout most of this backyard kitchen, a mosaic tile backsplash extends partially up the wall; behind the stove, however, it covers the entire surface for added protection from splatters.

RIGHT The marble countertop and backsplash in this outdoor kitchen matches the countertop inside the house, uniting them visually. And because the sink is under-mounted, cleanup is that much easier.

BELOW This blue flagstone is strong enough to be used on the floor and as a countertop. Just be sure that the countertop's overall weight isn't more than the base can withstand.

LEFT Built right into the countertop, a gas fire pit provides ambience and warmth. Positioned away from the working portion of this kitchen, it's a natural gathering spot, and doesn't get in the way of meal preparation.

décor

● ● ● ONCE YOU HAVE THE FOUNDATION OF AN OUTDOOR room in place, you can further shape its style with your décor. It should be as cozy and welcoming as any room you'd have inside, so try not to define it with the old "backyard" parameters. Instead, personalize it as you would any other space inside the house.

Items such as pillows, once the domain of indoors, are now available in weather- and water-resistant fabrics. The same holds true for outdoor rugs, which aren't the Astroturf®-like designs of yesteryear. Styles today are mildew resistant and colorfast, to avoid fading. You'll find everything from simple sisals to Oriental styles to modern geometric prints. To complete the room, set up an outdoor lamp or two, which have extra features that protect the electrical components from weather.

For a cohesive look, use your inside color palette and style to influence your selections outside. For example, if you have cool colors in the house, carry that scheme into the backyard. It will make the experience of moving from one to the other seamless and organic.

ABOVE An outdoor centerpiece should play up the natural surroundings. Here, an artful arrangement of stones and moss in a stunning black square vase is a simple but chic table topper.

ABOVE AND RIGHT This fire pit naturally
doubles as a dining table. Guests can sit
on the river rock flooring or settle in on the
nearby boulders. Or they can sit on either
side of the fire—on the table surface itself.

FACING PAGE Especially
in a densely wooded area,
white furnishings can
brighten up the space. Throw
pillows take their color cue
from a nearby flower garden,
making the whole space
cohesive yet striking.

more about...
TABLETOPS

plain wood picnic tables may have their appeal, but just because a table is outside doesn't mean it has to be of the picnic variety. The selection of styles and surface materials is great nowadays, allowing you to put your personal touch on your outdoor dining space.

New tables incorporate all of the usual suspects for durable materials: natural stone, faux stone, stainless steel, hardwoods, tile. But you could also opt to transform an existing piece by simply re-covering or replacing the top with any of the aforementioned materials.

When deciding, take time to think about where and how the table will be used. For example, if you're painting to transform the surface, choose an outdoor paint that is easy to wipe clean. Or if you want a tabletop made of a stone like granite, choose a light color so it won't be too hot for resting your arms. And when it comes to tiles, avoid white grout because it won't stay that way for long.

ABOVE A variety of decorative pillows adds a profusion of color and pattern to this sitting spot. One, ingeniously suspended from a rod, even serves as a backrest, making the space that much more comfortable.

LEFT An oversized chair and matching ottoman are particularly appealing outdoors. You have your choice of stretching out in put-your-feet-up comfort or curling up with a beverage or book.

Well-grounded neutral colors form the foundation of this pavilion living-dining area, pairing well with bright green pillows and table settings. The furnishings have a slightly modern vibe, thanks to clean lines and simple patterns that don't detract from the view.

more about...
CONCEALING ENTERTAINMENT SYSTEMS

having a TV or stereo outside can make a true living room out of your outdoor space. Problem is, these kinds of home electronics can be an eyesore. A few strategies for keeping gadgets out of sight include:

1. Put the controls for the stereo inside the house, with the speakers outside. That way you don't have to worry about hiding the main stereo unit.

2. Install speakers that can be buried in the soil, or surround them with plantings to obscure.

3. Buy outdoor products with built-in speakers. Many spas now have this feature, even allowing you to download a songlist from your iPod. This means no extra equipment needs to be outside.

4. Opt for a TV that electronically rises up from a TV cabinet. The television still needs to be made for outdoor use, so be sure it's weather- and water-resistant.

5. Mount the TV in the corner of a pavilion or gazebo, hanging from the ceiling so it's up and out of the way. This ensures it will not be the focal point of the room, but it can still easily be watched and enjoyed.

Set beneath a vine-covered pergola, this outdoor living area is simple yet stylish. Tangerine-colored seat cushions give the sofa fresh appeal while curtains—even when tied back— create a sense of privacy.

ABOVE Arched doorways allow sunlight to pour into this veranda, so the furniture's various fabrics and textures take on a decidedly rich personality.

LEFT Low-slung lounge chairs immediately conjure a relaxed atmosphere in this outdoor setting. Stripes in wide, neutral bands look modern and smart, their large scale well-suited to the oversized seating pieces.

•furniture and seating

The good news for those who live to be outdoors is that manufacturers have created furnishings that are just as comfortable and good-looking as anything you'd find inside. They're made with water-, mold-, and weather-resistant materials that are more tolerant of the elements. That said, too much exposure to rain can still result in mildew, and too much direct sunlight can eventually break down the fibers of even UV-resistant fabrics. To protect them, put furniture covers over top or set aside some weather-tight storage space for cushions and pillows.

Today's choices in outdoor furniture include metal (iron, aluminum, or steel), wood (teak, cedar, ipe, and others), as well as plastic—aka resin—which is used for, among other things, wicker look-alikes that are easier to care for than the real thing. In fact, before making any choice, consider the maintenance required. For example, teak furniture needs to be treated with teak sealer at least every year if you want to keep its natural color. And furniture with plentiful crevices can demand more elbow grease to get clean.

A Balinese-style wood sofa is made ultra comfortable with a collection of pillows in a variety of shapes and patterns, adding a softness to this Zenlike corner of the porch.

ABOVE Simple, unfussy furniture—like this pair of chairs—can make a dramatic impact. Set against a solid garden wall, the chairs' graceful shapes are boldly apparent.

LEFT Instead of relying solely on flowers for color and shape, you can introduce those attributes using furniture and planters. These chairs in summery hues, for example, instill a sunny disposition.

ABOVE Think of the exterior wall of a house as a potential backdrop for your furnishings. This rich chocolate color, for instance, is a handsome contrast to the vibrant orange loveseat and chair.

LEFT Even when it's part of a water feature, a low wall can provide additional seating and can even serve as a spot to set drinks, as long as there's not much splash from the fountain.

Not only is this console made of materials that can stand up to Mother Nature, but it's at its decorative best when the built-in perches beneath the tabletop are filled with lush potted plants.

The shape and color of this corner-turning bench is echoed by the stones. It is a prime spot to admire the fire pit. And, if needed, you could turn the space under the seat into storage for the cushions.

ABOVE On any outdoor furniture, don't underestimate the beauty and dirt-masking qualities of dark cushions. These coffee-colored chaises are quite dramatic in tandem with the mod bolster pillows.

RIGHT Making the most of this corner of the deck, built-in seating can accommodate a couple of people or a crowd. A profusion of pillows makes it a particularly appealing place to stretch out for an afternoon nap.

ABOVE This landscape takes advantage of natural nooks and turns them into sitting spots. The steep hill is an obvious draw for taking in the view, made more tempting with these built-in benches.

RIGHT This 10-foot concrete wall separates the grilling area from the rest of the patio. Directly in front of it, string-back folding chairs flank a planter—also made of concrete—providing a comfortable place to wait for dinner.

ABOVE Fitted with a soft low-voltage light, this pagoda lantern is both decorative and functional. Similar pieces are placed throughout this garden, wherever the views or the plantings are worthy of lingering.

ABOVE Layers of light create the most comfortable atmosphere, whether it's indoors or out. This lantern-like fixture specifically provides soft light for diners, while the recessed lighting in the ceiling generally illuminates the room.

lighting

● ● ● WHEN DECIDING WHERE TO PLACE YOUR LIGHTING fixtures, think of what you want to show off after dark, when much of your garden's beauty is no longer visible.

People often make the mistake of overlighting a garden area and ruining the ambience. For example, in most garden fixtures, 15 watts would suffice; simply use plenty of them for adequate illumination. In a kitchen or porch, though, where you need task lighting for food prep or for reading, more powerful fixtures should be placed strategically to offer targeted illumination.

To get the most out of lighting, take advantage of a variety of sources: overhead fixtures, table and floor lamps, spotlights aimed up from the ground, path lighting, sconces, and hanging lanterns. Together they can create a depth and texture that enhances a space.

You can also use your planting and material choices to give the impression of illumination. Light-colored fabrics and plants with variegated leaves reflect what light there is and, as a result, it has a greater effect.

make your own pierced-tin lantern

Here's a quick and easy way to bring light to your outdoor entertaining space. This pretty pierced-tin lantern requires a little skill, a bit of elbow grease, and a few old coffee cans. Make more than one with your kids and have fun at the same time.

SUPPLIES YOU WILL NEED
- Metal cans, labels removed
- Sand and water
- A variety of leaves with interesting, bold shapes
- Permanent black marker
- Sheets of vellum paper
- Masking tape
- Towel
- Hammer and nails
- Spray paint in white or off-white, as well as colors of your choice
- Votive candles

❶ PREPARE THE CAN. Fill the can with sand, add water, and place it in the freezer. The frozen mixture will give structure to the can and a surface against which to pound.

❷ MAKE THE TEMPLATE. Select a leaf that will fit the size of the can, and trace its shape with a permanent marker onto a long piece of vellum paper. Don't worry about details because only the basic shape will show up on the final product.

❸ POSITION THE DESIGN. When the water is completely frozen, take the can out of the freezer and tape the vellum paper tightly around the can, positioning the leaf outline.

❹ PUNCH THE HOLES. Rest the can on its side on a folded towel to keep it from rolling around and to protect the work surface. With a hammer and a sharp nail, punch holes though the paper and into the can along the lines of the design. Punch larger holes at the peaks in the leaf shape, at the intersections of veins, and along the stem to give some dimension. Change nails frequently, as they dull quickly after repeated punches. When the design is complete, remove the vellum paper, invert the can in a bowl, and allow it to thaw. Remove the sand and water, rinse the can well, and allow it to dry completely.

❺ PAINT THE LANTERN. Spray the inside of the lantern with white paint to diffuse the candlelight and give the lantern a brighter glow: A couple of quick shots of white or off-white spray paint aimed into the can from 3 to 4 inches above the opening. Then choose a color for the outside and spray on two light coats, allowing the paint to dry between coats. This paint is not only decorative but also offers a little protection from the elements if you leave your lanterns outside. Alternatively, you could skip the paint and just allow your lantern to rust over time. Insert the candle and light it with a long match.

This project originally appeared in Fine Gardening, *No. 87*

LEFT Placed along ceiling beams or woven into the spokes of an umbrella, outdoor string lights make a festive statement. Leave them up year-round and the space will always be ready for a party.

BELOW Putting a pergola over a brick patio further defines it as a room, but also provides a structure from which to hang lights. If your table is extra long, use two fixtures instead of one, so no one is left in the dark.

the problem with lighting outdoors from an energy-conservation standpoint is that outdoor lights tend to be on for longer than you actually need them to be. Maybe you flip on your front porch light when you leave the house at night, but it doesn't have to remain on the entire time you're gone. To cut back, set up a motion detector or timers so that lights come on either when you're coming up the pathway or at a time when they're actually helpful.

Installing CFLs (compact fluorescent lamps), which use 75 percent less energy than standard bulbs, or LEDs (light-emitting diodes)—which use up to 90 percent less energy and do really well outdoors, even in cold weather— also cuts down on electricity used.

You also may consider putting in solar-powered lights, which rely on the sun for energy. No matter what you choose, look for Energy Star– qualified outdoor fixtures. Some automatically shut off when the sun emerges; others are specifically made for cold weather (0 degrees and below). All are proven to be more energy efficient than traditional incandescent bulbs.

LEFT For outdoor lighting, take advantage of overhangs such as this one. The simple globe light is reminiscent of a full moon, beckoning you into the space.

fireplaces and fire pits

● ● ● BOTH COZY, NATURAL GATHERING SPOTS, fireplaces and fire pits actually have different personalities. A fireplace has a meditative quality, as everyone sits before it mesmerized by the flames. A fire pit, on the other hand, is intensely conversational, the group encircling the flames and facing one another across it.

Both can have important functions even when not lit. A fireplace often demands you take notice of its impressive construction, whether made of stone, brick, stucco, or concrete. A fire pit is usually less imposing, but often has a ledge or other features that allow you to use it as a bench or as a place to rest a drink and a book.

For both fireplaces and pits, prefab models are an inexpensive option; they can cost as little as a few hundred dollars. Or you can have one custom made to meld flawlessly with your landscape and furnishings.

ABOVE Built into the house's exterior wall, this fireplace provides warmth and appeal but doesn't demand the room's attention. The focus here is on the grouping of chairs and, consequently, on the conversation.

RIGHT An inviting fireplace is the undisputed focal point of this covered patio. Giving it even more attention, though, is strategically placed lighting that focuses squarely on the architectural elements.

Simple lines and materials are what make this gas fire pit so alluring. When large groups gather around, people can perch on the chairs, the edge of the pit, or even the nearby steps.

ABOVE AND RIGHT A full wall of folding doors allows guests to appreciate this fire pit, whether they're outdoors or in. So that the pit—and its flames—remain the central focus, the lighting that surrounds it is subtle.

This circular fire pit is positioned in one corner of a sky-high terrace. To make the most of the magnificent location, simple benches and a clear glass wall leave the views unobstructed.

RIGHT Taking advantage of an interior fireplace, an outdoor version is placed on the exterior side of the wall. This grand architectural element is the perfect starting point for a cozy conversation group.

LEFT Freestanding fireplaces are relatively inexpensive at home-improvement stores. The advantage is that they can be placed wherever you like; just be sure there are no trees or powerlines overhead.

Evocative of chairs gathered around a campfire, this area has the same simplicity but is much more refined. The concrete wall defines the space and disguises the pool equipment behind it.

To make the most of outdoor living, this wood-burning fireplace has an attached pizza oven. It also becomes part of the décor, as the fabric choices play up the coral-colored stone and chimneys.

ABOVE A dining area set near an outdoor fireplace allows guests to linger longer into the night, as the flames buffer the chill in the air. In the same way, an outdoor fireplace can also extend the outdoor-dining season.

LEFT The flagstone used on the floor of this outdoor living room continues right up the fireplace, creating design continuity and complementing the color of the house.

garden spaces

• ○ ○

A GARDEN CAN TRANSFORM A BACKYARD FROM BORING AND BARREN to colorful and intriguing. With various leaf shapes and flower silhouettes, it can provide texture; and different color palettes can establish a variety of moods. A garden can even create adventure, taking visitors on a beautiful journey full of surprises.

The key is to carefully sketch out your plantings on graph paper to design your overall scheme in advance. (Impulse buys at the garden center can lead to an unsuccessful, disjointed garden.) As you plan, keep the basics in mind: Tall plants in back, shorter plants in front. And try to stimulate as many of the senses as possible: Fragrant plants for scent, beautiful views for sight, a dining table where you can taste, a water fountain or birdbath for sound, and wonderful textures on furnishings and stonework for touch.

If you live in a climate that prevents you from sitting outside during the colder months, position your garden within clear view from the house so you can enjoy it even from indoors. And choose plantings that evolve with the seasons, creating different vistas throughout the year.

A garden arch, overflowing with roses, beckons visitors toward a table for two. Considering the view of the garden as you enter is as important as how it looks once you're inside.

garden rooms

● ● ● A GARDEN ROOM CAN FUNCTION AS A SPACE TO accomodate nearly any need. It can be a place to eat, to read, to play, to socialize, to find solitude—or all of the above. Ask yourself what you and your family want out of it to determine which path to take.

Also think about the views you'll have from this outdoor room. Give some thought to what kind of sun exposure it will have throughout the year, too, so you can determine what the best plantings would be.

How you establish the borders of your garden room can also have a great impact. For example, a gravel floor clearly delineates the space and maintains a naturalistic feel. Plus, there's something soothing about the "crunch" you hear as your feet pass over the surface. Hedges or fences, on the other hand, can create natural walls that add to the sense of seclusion. Or if you prefer a more open layout, use shorter walls or shrubs to frame "borrowed" landscapes, which are beautiful views in the distance.

Anyone who occupies these simple chaises are treated to another sensory pleasure, the soothing trickle of water from the nearby fountain.

ABOVE Hedges and an ivy-covered wall define the far edge of this garden room. A bricked floor does its part to further establish the border.

LEFT A small bistro table and chairs makes this shaded area ideal for stealing a few quiet moments with a friend, proving that—even with just the basics—a garden room can feel like a special retreat.

more about...
BONSAI PLANTS

@ popular art form in Japan, bonsai is an elegant option for outdoor spaces. Trees that normally grow to be full-size, such as elm, maple, and boxwood, are trained to grow in small containers, through regular trimming and pruning.

Bonsai requires patience and steady maintenance, but delivers big rewards, with inspiring shrunken landscapes you'd otherwise only find on a larger scale out in nature. If you care for them properly, they can last for decades.

Because bonsai is maintained in small containers, people often make the mistake of attempting to turn them into indoor plants. But since few will survive inside, they are better suited to a garden room.

Under the shade of a sprawling tree, four Adirondack chairs and a cherry-red bench encircle a small table, setting a decidedly tranquil scene, ever-ready for a picnic.

A water fountain mounted on an exterior wall leads the eye directly to this sitting spot—an oversize wicker chair that beckons you to sit down and relax.

create privacy screening

❶ FILTER VIEWS WITH COLUMNAR TREES.
Columnar, or fastigiate, trees stay relatively
narrow as they grow taller and also provide a
strong vertical element in the landscape. Use
evergreen plant material where you want year-
round privacy and deciduous material where
enclosure in the summer is more important.

❷ MAKE THE MOST OF ELEVATION CHANGES.
Refocus the view from the neighboring buildings
to the center of the yard. Changes in elevation
create the illusion of more space, so create a
sunken garden. For example, dig an area about
14 feet by 28 feet to a depth of 14 inches to
create a patio surrounded by a seat wall. Using
the dirt from the excavation, create a berm, or
mound, ranging in height from 18 to 24 inches
above the original grade. As soon as you take
the first step down into the sunken garden,
your focus is on the patio and on the garden.

**❸ USE FREESTANDING TRELLIS PANELS
TO SCREEN THE VIEW.** You can intersperse
freestanding trellis panels 8 feet tall and 4 feet
wide with columnar pine trees (*Pinus strobus*
'Fastigiata', Zones 4–9) to partially screen the
view. In the winter, they still block the view.
The panels can allow you to catch glimpses
into a neighbor's garden, while still giving some
privacy. Zoning codes often allow a trellis to be
built at a greater height than a fence can be.

**❹ STAGGER PLANT MATERIAL FOR MUTUAL
PRIVACY.** To decide how to create some privacy,
sit in each of the seating areas in your garden
and look toward your neighbor's house. Planting
in a staggered, or triangular, pattern often will
limit the view without requiring a solid hedge.
This grouping can also block the view of
your own driveway or garage, which makes a
dramatic difference in the feel of the garden.

*This project by Rosalind Reed originally appeared
in* Fine Gardening *No. 90*

RIGHT With some stone pavers, a wicker furniture set, and a little strategic landscaping, a corner of the yard can go from unused lawn to practical garden room.

BELOW A garden room becomes a Zen escape with cushioned chairs, a fire pit, and pebbles that make a soothing sound underfoot. The solid fence is softened, too, with a virtual wall of greenery.

ABOVE In the center of this combination bench-planter, greenery breaks up the expansive hardscape. And there's more visual interest in its façade, which is decked out in a geometric pattern of stone.

ABOVE A rough-hewn wood bench is distinctive enough to be eye-catching but still blends in with its surroundings. A garden with seating instantly becomes a space in which you want to spend time.

The simplicity of this seating area is what makes it so striking. Two trees anchor the space, framing a bench and an oversized container. Inexpensive pea gravel distinguishes the area from the nearby brick path.

Set on a concrete pad just off the beaten path, this nook feels like a magical escape—a restorative place for tea for two or solitary contemplation.

ABOVE A path that wends its way around clusters of plantings creates a dynamic garden room. In the center of it all, a copper fountain is a soothing accent.

LEFT A wooden bench at the edge of this backyard is set close enough to a fountain to appreciate its comforting trickle but far enough away to take in the garden's splendor in its entirety.

paths, walkways, and flooring

The materials you choose for paths, walkways, and flooring can set the mood for an entire outdoor room, if not the whole yard. They can add color and texture to a garden space, working in conjunction with plants to achieve just the right look.

The selection is almost endless, as manufacturers come up with ever more durable, beautiful products. You'll find manmade materials like concrete pavers and brick, as well as natural stone, such as slate and granite.

Whatever you choose, be sure to keep safety in mind. Polished or honed stones, for instance, can be particularly slick in wet weather. Also consider your lifestyle; if you tend to traipse around barefoot, choose a material that when exposed to the sun won't be too hot for walking.

Stone is durable and can be cut to fit a specific space, but different types of stone can have very different looks: Flagstone has a casual, informal appearance, while precisely cut rectangles of bluestone take on a more traditional air. But stone can be expensive. To cut down on shipping costs, look into local quarry options, which are also a more earth-friendly choice.

Perhaps most durable of all is concrete, which can be molded, stained, or stamped to mimic any type of stone or brick on your property. It also can be quite affordable because it can be poured and then customized, rather than cut and placed as individual pavers.

The weekend do-it-yourselfer can easily apply a stain or paint to concrete to produce a variety of color effects. But customizing it with stamps can require a little more expertise, as the wet cement demands you work quickly.

Flagstone serves as both pathway and floor for this oasis of a garden space. The bench is a draw in large part because of the view it offers of the well-planned yard.

ABOVE This garden room is softened with a carpet of grass, broken up by a meandering path that leads to the seating area. More hardscape, including concrete planters, also provides a reprieve from the green.

RIGHT Pebbles embedded in some of these concrete pavers echo nearby clusters of smooth river stones. Meanwhile, chamomile is a soft and versatile groundcover that releases a transfixing aroma.

LEFT Succulents, such as this delicate sedum, make a beautiful, low-maintenance groundcover. Here, it's bordered by cut chrysanthemums that add a festive punch of color.

BELOW Four concrete planters define a small garden "room" at the corner of this pathway. There's sufficient space for a small bistro table and chairs without obstructing passersby.

FACING PAGE Flagstone broken up with tufts of green softens the transition from garden to hardscape, making the entire space feel like one cohesive room.

g a l l e r y

paths

Think of a path as a place to be rather than just a way of getting from one spot to another. It can heighten the interest and suspense through its journey, as well as through its materials and surrounding plantings.

ABOVE Concrete steps in various thicknesses.

RIGHT Large concrete slabs.

ABOVE Brick steps to a rose garden.

LEFT Voluptuous plantings line a path for more mystery.

RIGHT Wood-block steps.

BELOW Blue flagstone.

RIGHT A bright white gate stands out against the greenery of the garden and trees in the distance. It serves as both a focal point and a destination, its shape mimicking the nearby circular water feature.

garden passageways

A garden entryway can welcome you with varying degrees of privacy, intrigue, and suspense. Placed around an entry, arbors, gates, fences, and container plantings instantly indicate that visitors are either going into or coming out of a special place. The style of the passageway can even give you a hint as to the style of the garden beyond. For example, a gate made of rustic sticks—and bound with twine—adds an air of informality, while a stone gate with hedges lets you know that what lies beyond is private, intended for only those who are invited.

Keep in mind how your gate will look not just as you approach the space, but while you're actually sitting in the garden on the other side. Gates and arches are more than mere welcoming features. They can also frame views as you peer in or out.

ABOVE A cutout in a gate or garden door allows visitors to peek inside—and can add a whimsical element, too.

Walls give a room defined boundaries, but can close it off from external light and views. Here, two wood-grid gates allow in a little of both, breaking up the expanse of stucco.

LEFT Although this gate leads to nowhere, it's a destination at the end of this pathway and offers a bit of quirky garden humor.

LEFT A bamboo gate conveys that what lies within is a calming, natural retreat. A chair, immediately visible upon entrance, is another welcoming gesture.

RIGHT A Southwestern-style adobe wall is set off by a pair of weathered turquoise-and-yellow doors. And since there are no slats for peeking at the other side, it provides a great deal of privacy.

FACING PAGE Antique Indian palace doors form a grand entrance to this garden, with greenery forming the adjacent "walls." They were positioned with views in mind, to stimulate the senses both coming and going.

RIGHT A quaint circle of white-picket fencing surrounds this sweet flower garden. Complete with a pathway that leads you through it, the setting is even more striking amid a grassy lawn.

ABOVE Expand your options by using conventional garden objects in unconventional ways. Set in a garden of blooms, this birdbath-turned-flower-pot fits right in.

•flower gardens

Flower gardens are a delight, adding color and texture to what could otherwise be an uninterrupted expanse of green lawn. To create a truly lush garden, you'll need to do some planning beforehand. First, test the soil to determine what supplemental nutrients it may need. And research the plants you're interested in to find out their spatial needs, shade/sun requirements, and necessary maintenance.

Even in a well-shaded garden, you can bring in the impression of sunlight with lighter-colored flowers and plants with variegated foliage. In fact, the strategic placement of color can make a difference throughout the yard by tricking the eye. When paired with light colors, for example, darker hues add depth and prevent a flower garden from appearing flat. In very sunny spots, pastel blooms can become washed out and lose their impact; in shady corners, dark blues and purples won't stand out.

In any garden, plan for some open space to give the eye a breather; it might be in the form of a patio, a patch of lawn, or a swath of groundcover. The pattern in which you plant your flowers can also be used to great effect. Straight lines lend a formal air, while curves establish a more organic flow.

Wooden tripod trellises gives this garden an extra dimension, encouraging flowering vines to grow upward. Throughout, the garden is contained in raised beds, leaving the pathways clear.

PLANTING TO CONSERVE

When choosing plants for your garden, it makes economic and environmental sense to opt for ones that don't demand an abundance of water, fertilizer, or pesticides. For example, native plants are better adapted to their environs than exotic plants are, so they often require less maintenance. This makes them a wiser choice for shrinking your carbon footprint, as well as for making your yardwork chores less time-consuming.

Native plants can also help restore the local ecology. The insects, pollinators, and birds that evolved with the plants often return, finding both food and shelter. To learn what plants are native to your area, consult your state's native plant society or use the native plant database at www.wildflower.org/plants.

Not all native plants are low-maintenance, however. That's where drought-tolerant varieties come in; they aren't necessarily indigenous, but they don't need to be watered frequently and can typically thrive on rainwater alone.

Both native and drought-tolerant plants are good ecological choices over a conventional lawn. Turf grass is a monoculture—which means there's only one species of plant—but nature favors diversity and is constantly trying to add more plants, such as weeds, to your lawn. The beauty of native and drought-tolerant plants is that they avoid battling each other for resources.

LEFT AND BELOW Drought-tolerant grasses require less water than turf grass and no mowing, either. Available in a variety of sizes and colors, they can give paths or steps more textural dimension.

FACING PAGE Replacing turf grass with flowering plants can be both water-wise and environmentally smart. Lawns require about 80 percent more water and hours more maintenance.

FACING PAGE A flower garden is framed by white arched trellises so that, depending on where you're coming from, the perspectives are continuously evolving but are always stunning.

LEFT A tucked-away path bisects this flower garden, providing enough room to walk through without detracting from the dynamic colors.

BELOW Swaths of grass can serve as much-needed visual relief when set beside a riot of colors and textures. These grassy paths also function as a border, further defining the garden area.

container plantings

● ● ● YOU CAN ALTER THE ENTIRE PERSONALITY OF A space by changing out or adding container plantings, bringing in new textures, colors, and shapes. And this kind of transformation is one of the least expensive ways to give the garden a quick makeover.

When planning your container design, determine if it will be seen from all angles, or just the front. If it's the latter, put taller plants in back; if the former, make sure there are appealing vignettes from every side.

Think in terms of groupings of threes or fives, in both number of plants and number of containers. It's a fundamental principle of design: Using odd numbers in a composition is more visually appealing.

You can rely on the plantings you choose to add new colors to an outdoor room, or to reflect what is already happening. The character of the container—whether it's tall and shiny or short and heavily textured—also contributes visual interest.

To test the success of your design, take a snapshot of what you've planted, then turn the photo upside down. If the composition is good, it will look just as appealing as it does right side up.

Always consider how a container planting will look year-round. Nandina bamboo, the tall plant in the center, has fall berries and foliage, which harmonize nicely with the plum tones of the cascading sweet potato vine (far right).

LEFT Because they require less water and have bold sculptural forms, succulents make wonderful container plants. This grouping of three succulent-filled pots shows off the plants' varied colors, too

BELOW This stunning container planting is a cascade of beauty. The impactful design doesn't rely on a diverse color palette but, instead, on variations in texture and form.

create a lush container planting

1 To determine if you need to supplement your garden with container plantings, take photos of it in black-and-white. If it looks like one dark mass, it might benefit from some lighter colors to add tonal value. In other words, your garden should show its diversity in black-and-white just as well as it does in color.

2 Choose plants in threes or fives, since odd numbers are more visually appealing. At least one should be the star, the centerpiece. Another should be filler to flesh out the pot and complement the star. And a third should tumble out of the pot to add drama and verticality. Look for a balance of textures, shapes, and colors.

3 Do you want your container garden to be visible at night? If so, include lighter-colored foliage and flowers that will reflect the moonlight.

4 Use the right type of potting soil for the plants you've chosen. Succulents, for instance, require a greater percentage of sand.

5 Feed your plants often with a slow-release food and use a granular feeder such as osmocote.

ABOVE This container planting and its identical companion (out of view) flank a back entry to make it more dramatic. They frame the view and demand that you take notice.

RIGHT A collection of container plantings —in front of and on top of a garden wall—softens the architectural elements. A handsome concrete trough and faucet make easy work of watering them all.

RIGHT Plants that bloom in the off-season are a welcome treat when everything else is dormant. This Christmas cactus produces feathery, gentle pink blossoms right around the holidays.

LEFT Greenery is often used under windows in freestanding planters or window boxes. Here, though, plants also flank the window halfway up, the reflective quality of their leaves not unlike sconces.

BELOW The beauty of this container planting lies in its simplicity, befitting the contemporary home. There's no voluminous greenery here, just the juxtaposition of false aralia and a fish hook plant growing in opposite directions.

RIGHT Each of these 'Tropicana' cannas is dramatic in its own right, but lining the perimeter of an outdoor pavilion with them—all in matching planters—multiplies the effect.

more about...
SMALL-SCALE CONTAINERS

p otted plantings are like gardens in miniature, so when you put them in even smaller pots, they become the tiniest of landscapes. Their size makes them mutable components in a composition of your choosing: Several small containers can be clustered together, so that the grouping forms a cohesive scene; or they can stand alone on a dining table as a centerpiece or on a side table as an accent.

Cut flowers can die after a matter of days, but small potted plants can last well through the season. When choosing plants, think about the colors that will appear behind them, whether from a wall or hedge. Pick plants with leaves and blooms that will stand out against that background, and ones that will thrive outdoors without much care.

LEFT A bright yellow container provides a welcome pop of color, the tall plants within seemingly doubling its stature and presence.

RIGHT Dwarf trees such as this Japanese maple can thrive in a container. Thanks to a northern exposure and a shade-providing overhang, this is a particularly amenable spot.

When allowed to grow to full size and positioned en masse
to create contrasts in texture, vegetable plants can become
a painterly masterpiece.

themed gardens

●●● CREATING A GARDEN WITH A COMMON THEME IS A
terrific way to inject it with your personality. Look to your own interests and
hobbies to fashion a garden that suits you perfectly.

If you like to travel, for instance, emulate your favorite destination—an
English garden, a tropical theme, or succulents reminiscent of the Southwest. Or theme the
garden around a favorite color, designing the entire plant palette in varying tones of a single
hue: purple, pink, even shades of green. Or bring in a naturalistic theme, using elements such
as water gardens or stone gardens. You might even design your garden around the theme of
bounty, growing vegetables like leafy greens that can be both beautiful and delicious.

LEFT AND ABOVE This meditative courtyard space has many Japanese components: A marble bowl in the shape of a lotus (left) has great significance in that culture, as do dark river rocks that are arranged to mimic water flowing.

ATTRACTING WILDLIFE

With the right food, water, and shelter, wildlife will be easily attracted to your garden. Make sure you have plenty of each, and you'll be enjoying birds and creatures year-round.

Native plants provide the berries and seeds that the indigenous wildlife needs to survive. Use logs, bushes, rocks, or even birdhouses to let animals know you've got housing for them. Ponds are great for animals drawn to the water, and will attract them almost immediately. Other water elements, such as water fountains and birdbaths, will bring small birds and insects to your yard. If you want hummingbirds in particular, choose red flowers (which they love) and plants that produce nectar. Butterflies also like

flowers with nectar, like asters, azalea, coneflower, and goldenrod. The more colorful your garden is, the more likely they are to visit.

Also use natural, sustainable gardening methods. Non-organic fertilizers and pesticides not only kill the insects and pests that wildlife likes to eat, but they can also harm animals.

If your backyard meets certain criteria that make it hospitable to animals, you can have it certified by the National Wildlife Federation as an official wildlife habitat. Go to www.nwf.org/backyard/certify.cfm for more information.

LEFT, TOP, AND ABOVE In this Tahitian-themed backyard, there's a stretch of sand and a collection of tropical plants in lieu of a lawn. A raised concrete water fountain is even topped with an island idol.

LEFT Any garden put in a raised planter, like this one, which is filled with vegetables and herbs, is easier to maintain because there's no need to bend over.

RIGHT Rocks and boulders can make as much of a statement in your yard as conventional plantings. Magnifying the sound of a sheet fountain flowing from above, these rocks help create a truly tranquil space.

GROW A KNOT GARDEN

dating back to the 16th century, knot gardens incorporate contrasting foliage colors to give the impression that the plants are weaving through one another, creating a beautiful living tapestry. Evergreens and herbs are best suited for these gardens; those that are short in stature or low-growing are easiest to clip (how often you do so depends on the plant). And this type of garden can fit into even small spaces, because it's ideally about six feet in diameter.

Knot gardens are even more appealing from a distance, as the pattern becomes more lucid. Looking out from a second-story window, for instance, often offers the best vantage point.

As lovely as they are, they do require frequent pruning and trimming. But it's easy to fall in love with the fragrance, beauty, and delicious possibilities, making the work well worth it.

1. First, make a drawing of your design on graph paper, using each square to represent one plant.

2. To map out the pattern, push a 2-foot wooden stake into the ground where each plant will be placed. Then label each with the type of plant you choose, indicating where the colors change. Wrap twine around each stake and string it to the next, so you can better see how the design will take shape.

3. Plant the evergreens and herbs close together so they appear to be one contiguous line.

4. In the center of the "knots" you can put pea gravel to provide contrast with the green of the plants. Or you can plant clusters of herbs.

ABOVE AND RIGHT The diagram shown above takes shape in a real-life herb knot garden. Look closely, and you can see the subtle texture and color changes that from afar are quite striking.

FAR LEFT A sculptural water fountain welcomes guests to this outdoor living space while discreetly covering an electrical box, too. At night, a spotlight aimed directly at it keeps the attention squarely on the water feature.

NEAR LEFT The gurgling water coming from the spouts in this pond can be turned off and on, and can even be set up so the water flow is triggered by movement as someone passes by.

water fountains

● ● ● AN AQUATIC SOUNDTRACK FOR YOUR GARDEN, A water fountain can create a soothing trickle, gentle spray, or more energized gush. This can be especially useful if you're trying to drown out noise from the street or neighbors. Also think of the visual benefits, as a fountain is akin to jewelry for the garden. It can be used to redirect the focus, add new shapes and colors, or conceal unflattering elements.

When it comes to fountain styles, some are fed from an attached pond, some are wall-mounted, and some are freestanding and recirculate within themselves. A fountain's personality can be anything from traditional and regal to modern and sleek to earthy and naturalistic.

Many manufactured fountains are made of fiberglass, which is lightweight and easy to disassemble for cleaning and storage. However, fiberglass can look fake and can chip or fade over time. Stone fountains tend to be more substantial, but are also pricier, as are ceramic and metal. Before making your choice, be sure it's equipped to handle your climate. For example, it should be frost-resistant if you have cold winters.

ABOVE Protruding from an ivy-covered wall, a waterspout in the shape of a fish creates a soothing trickling sound as the water lands in the basin below.

LEFT Surrounded by herbs and feathery grasses, a stone Japanese water bowl—called a tsukabai—is filled by a bamboo spout. In Japan, you would use the ladle to rinse your hands and mouth before entering a temple.

sculpture and garden décor

● ● ● ONE OF THE BEST WAYS TO PERSONALIZE an outdoor space is with décor that speaks to your heart. A small stone statue of a girl reading a book might be a special nod to the librarian who lives in the house. Likewise, an avid birdwatcher might incorporate sculptures of sparrows, woodpeckers, or finches here and there.

There are two schools of thought in terms of placement. On one hand, you might situate your statuary out in the open, enticing guests to come in for a closer look. Just as effective, though, is hiding something to add intrigue. The joy of discovering an angelic white cherub peeking out from tall flowers can put a smile on anyone's face. To mix it up, consider placing some artwork in clusters, and others on their own.

Antiques, like this 19th-century gypsy cart, can often be repurposed as garden furniture. Adding a cushion with an exotic pattern makes it more comfortable without detracting from its character.

LEFT AND BELOW An antique chrysanthemum doorknocker was the inspiration for this concrete pad. Embedded in the "petals" are old Indian cooking pots, which were pressed into the concrete when it was still wet.

ABOVE A simple coat of paint on a wall can make your plantings pop. When compared with the adjacent white wall, the red one clearly adds more definition and dimension to these grasses.

RIGHT A giant wood Ganesh—a Hindu god and remover of obstacles—is adorned here with a fresh orchid necklace and oversize red umbrella. The pattern on the headdress even inspired the plantings and stonework below.

ABOVE An antique woodcarving, durable enough to be used outdoors, dresses up this doorframe.

LEFT An old copper pot filled with water and floating Gerbera daisies generates instant elegance. Think of decorating a garden as you would a dining table, using cut flowers to add festive flourishes.

pools and play spaces

●●●

ONE OF THE BEST THINGS ABOUT A BACKYARD IS THAT IT'S AN IDEAL place for play. And nothing says "play" for people of all ages more than a pool. The options are almost endless—from geometric to naturalistic shapes, from designs that stand out prominently to those that blend in with the surroundings.

Almost every yard is a candidate for a pool, no matter how small or oddly shaped the space may be. When determining placement, consider your privacy. Positioning a pool behind trees, bushes, or some other type of screening material will help block your view of the neighbors (and vice versa).

Before embarking on a pool project, consult with your builder on construction requirements. Excavation equipment often needs ample space and a clear path in order to dig up your yard. For safety reasons, don't position a pool under power lines. And to keep maintenance and cleaning to a minimum, also avoid placing it under trees that shed their leaves.

For small children, grassy areas and play equipment can make the backyard a personal amusement park. The creative examples of jungle gyms and play areas in this chapter set imaginations in motion. For older kids and adults, there are basketball, tennis, and other sport courts, all of which can provide endless hours of family entertainment and together time. Even the most basic additions can make an impact—perhaps a simple tire swing or a grassy patch just large enough for a game of croquet. It doesn't require much to turn a backyard into a fun zone.

Sometimes the simplest playthings make the biggest impact on a child. Suspended from the sturdy branches of an old tree, a swing stimulates the imagination in ways video games never will.

pools

● ● ● A POOL IN THE BACKYARD IS A WONDERFUL TREAT. IT NOT only serves as a place to cool off, play around, or get some exercise, but it's also a great spot for entertaining.

When considering where to place the pool, make sure it's close enough to the house, or a pool house, that you can come and go easily—for bathroom breaks, snacks, or just a respite from the sun. Also consider its exposure to the sun. In hot climates, you may want a pool in the shade; in cooler areas, you might want the warmth of the sun to help heat the water.

Even in a small lot, a pool can be customized—by size and shape—to meet all of your needs. You don't have to have plentiful acreage to enjoy the indulgence of cool water on a hot day.

ABOVE AND RIGHT A pool and spa adopt the look of this Mediterranean-style home. A striking border of tile further defines it from the adjacent grassy area, which can function as a pool deck or place for games.

FACING PAGE A series of formal container plantings define cozy gathering spots. Small conversation groupings often make people more comfortable mingling.

ABOVE AND RIGHT Part of this multi-level pool deck is made of sturdy ipe wood while the other is peach-colored sandstone. Built-in water features include a waterfall wall and spouts, which are powered by the filter motor so don't require additional energy.

LEFT From the bricked deck, sunbathers can take in the view of the pool—complete with whimsical waterspouts and a spa at one end—as well as the elevated garden beyond.

Not only does the design of this infinity pool eliminate any disruption between it and the magnificent scenery, but the water also reflects the views, making them that much more impactful.

INFINITY POOLS

i nfinity-edge pools, also referred to as vanishing-edge and negative-edge pools, are the ultimate in luxury. Because the sides appear to meld with the landscape, whatever lies beyond the water's edge becomes the focal point, so be sure it's something worthy of that extra attention.

In fact, the added expense of an infinity pool may not make sense unless you have a fabulous vista. With an ocean view in the distance,

for instance, the pool can look as if it's part of the larger body of water, bringing that magnificent scenery closer to home.

This type of pool is best for a home on a slope, or where the pool will somehow be elevated. The water that spills over the vanishing edge is recycled back into the pool but requires specific equipment, so be sure your pool contractor is experienced with this type of setup.

On any given day, you have plenty of options here: a spot for dining on the far end, a comfortably cushioned chaise with a built-in canopy, and a spa with an amazing view of the pool and the landscape.

LEFT The curved edges of this infinity pool and spa mirror the shape of the arches on a nearby terrace, a design decision that was made to enhance and frame the view from inside.

ABOVE The water level here appears to come right up to the top of the pool, because it cascades off the far edge into a basin, where it is then recirculated.

LEFT Even a small backyard can accommodate a pool. This compact 8 foot by 29 foot-lap pool, mere steps from the back doors, is convenient enough that it gets used frequently.

BELOW To make room for a pool in this backyard, decking was limited to one end. A surrounding fence is required in many municipalities, so check your local ordinances before building.

This deck, cantilevered over one end of the pool, allows occupants to look out from above. Meanwhile, palm fronds form a natural shield from the sweltering sun.

gallery

organically-shaped pools

A pool lined with boulders, rocks, and plantings can look like something straight out of nature—more like a pond or lake than a man-made creation. This style is ideal for homes that are less formal, especially when a surrounding garden takes on a more organic personality or when the pool sits amid a stand of trees.

You can complement the look with waterfalls and other water features, giving the pool a convincingly natural appearance and sound; trickling water is soothing, indeed. Keep in mind, however, that if you place plants or trees near the water, there will probably be more maintenance required, too.

2

1

3

1 A small pool looks like a water hole amid rocky terrain.

2 A pond-like pool complements the linear nature of the steps.

3 A man-made rock formation creates a natural-looking waterfall.

4 Plantings and stonescaping mimic a setting straight out of nature.

5 An amoeba-shaped pool has a polished, contemporary aesthetic.

5

4

Furniture that is more about living in comfort than getting a tan is also at home alongside a pool, especially if you tend to entertain outdoors. A party is always more fun when there's a cushiony place to sit.

poolside seating

● ● ● EVEN WITH A POOL IN YOUR BACKYARD, YOU'LL likely spend more time hanging out on the side than in the water itself. That means you'll want to appoint the deck or surrounding area with comfortable seating. It can be something that blends in with the surroundings, like a built-in bench, or something that stands out as a work of art, like a contemporary chair with colorful cushions. It can be a chaise for lounging in the sun, or a complete living room set for casual gatherings. It can even be a dining table and chairs, so poolside meals are easy—and, therefore, frequent.

To decide what type of seating is right for you, think about how you will use the pool. Is it an escape, an opportunity to relax and read? If so, you want comfy pieces on which you can put up your feet. Or is it a place for parties? If that's the case, you'll want small groupings of tables and chairs. Or perhaps you want some of each.

ABOVE These sun loungers are made with tear-proof polyester and have an anti-UV powder coating, important characteristics for furniture that will be sitting outside for months at a time.

LEFT These chaises are constructed of reclaimed teak, making them environmentally friendly. Because they're lightweight, they can easily be pulled back onto the covered patio during inclement weather or in the off-season.

more about...
OUTDOOR CUSHIONS

When it comes to pillows and cushioned pads for outdoors, fabric choices are almost as wide-ranging as they are for indoors. New technology brings us durable UV-, stain-, and water-resistant options in all manner of colors and patterns.

Not all outdoor fabrics are created equal, however. For instance, the color is more durable—and long-lasting—when the individual fibers are dyed and then woven, as opposed to fabric that's woven and then dyed or printed. Check to see if both sides of your fabric look the same, with the same colors and patterns if so, it's the sturdier option.

The best, and first, thing to do is thoroughly read care instructions before purchasing, so you know what the maintenance routine will entail. Many outdoor fabrics can be cleaned by simply wiping away dirt and dust with a damp cloth or soft brush. And be sure to clean up spills immediately; regular cleaning will prevent mildew, too. If the pillow cover is removable, you can probably throw it in the washer. But don't put it in the dryer because it can shrink.

ABOVE A wood daybed, complete with an island-inspired thatched roof, creates a paradise for lounging out of the sun. An abundance of pillows makes the space even more inviting.

This bench sits beside the pool, but is light enough to be moved to an outdoor fireplace area when the homeowners entertain. Furniture with multiple uses like this maximizes both space and money.

Any dining area, poolside or not, should be placed off the beaten path. This one sits just beyond the brick walkway on a bed of pea gravel and is further defined by Cyprus container plantings.

ABOVE A pergola swathed in weatherproof fabric lets in as much light as you like. Lengths of it suspended from the rafters can be pulled back and forth while shades on the sides roll up and down.

RIGHT When choosing poolside seating, give some thought to how many people will typically gather—and how they'll use the area. A double chaise, for instance, easily accommodates two people, or one who sprawls out for afternoon naps.

spas

● ● ● WITH THEIR WARM AND SOOTHING NATURE, SPAS SEEM TO make daily concerns evaporate right along with the steam. And because a spa is often connected to the pool, you can easily slip from one to the other for a therapeutic water massage. If you plan to join the two, installing them at the same time will cost less than if you were to add each one separately.

Left out in the open, a spa allows you to take in the stars while enjoying an evening soak. Or it can be put in a separate structure, such as a gazebo, enclosed for a sense of privacy.

If you want your spa to be the focal point of the backyard, surround it with a bar or put a fireplace nearby (prefab models often offer these features). Alternatively, to make it a surprising indulgence, tuck it into the landscape more discreetly.

ABOVE The circular shape of this spa is repeated in the nearby fire pit, creating a rhythm that's inherently soothing and relaxing.

RIGHT This square spa matches the formality of the pool and the architecture of the house. Its materials are also shared by the home and pool, thus establishing design continuity throughout the yard.

This spa has an ample ledge, allowing people to sit and converse with those in the water. When not being used as a spa, a telescopic jet transforms it into a fountain—and a brand-new focal point.

ABOVE A variety of materials—from smooth sand-colored pavers to rough-hewn stone to intricate mosaic tile—make this spa visually interesting. An extra-wide ledge adds practicality by providing additional seating.

BELOW The controls of this spa are conveniently located on the spa itself, so there's no need to get out of the water to adjust the jets.

Moving back and forth between a cold plunge pool and a hot spa can be invigorating. Because children reside nearby, these are cordoned off with a removable fence.

LEFT This spa, which overflows into the pool to create a peaceful waterfall, can be just as easily accessed from the pool as it can from the deck.

RIGHT With plant-filled urns at all four corners, this spa is bordered by the same sand-colored stone that surrounds the adjacent pool, making them both stand out amid the verdant grass.

FACING PAGE A flagstone deck leads right up to the edge of this in-ground spa, which has a cut-out on one side that's just big enough to move through to the pool.

pool houses

●●● THE MAIN FUNCTION OF A POOL HOUSE IS A home away from home, a place that provides a bathroom, a shower, storage space, and even entertainment areas. It can also double as guest quarters or an office and, in colder climates, can house the pool itself.

Before choosing a style, do a little research about the architecture of your primary residence. Consider designs common to the era in which it was built, factoring in the materials and colors used elsewhere in your backyard landscape.

But don't be afraid to take a few risks, either; in such a small structure, making an architectural statement can be exhilarating. You might rely on one of today's prefab structures, which are more sophisticated than ever before. There are also many books about pool house design that you can use as a starting point when working with a designer or architect.

ABOVE AND LEFT This small pool house is reminiscent of a Japanese hot sauna. Wooden sliding doors even open to reveal a low table with Japanese-style seating.

FACING PAGE A covered patio expands the living space of this pool house while providing options for both indoor and outdoor entertaining.

This pool house is original to the residence, complete with tilework from the 1920s and an awning that is also inspired by that era. But even if you're building a new pool house, it can look as if it's always been there.

RIGHT Local stone used to build this cupola-topped pool house gives it a native feel and an eco-friendly advantage, too: There's no long-distance shipping involved.

BELOW With floor-to-ceiling glass doors, this pool house has excellent visual connectivity with the outdoors, and there's a greater sense of space indoors, too.

outdoor showers

●●● WITH ITS ROOTS DEEP-SEATED IN PRACTICALITY, AN outdoor shower is the perfect place to rinse off sand, chlorine, or dirt before going back into the house. But it also has spiritual benefits, as scrubbing up in the great outdoors seems somehow more refreshing.

Placing the shower along the side of the house not only allows easy access to the necessary pipes, but it also eliminates having to traipse great distances once you're clean. And for privacy purposes, think beyond conventional solutions; vines or other plant materials, for instance, can serve as supplementary screens. Finally, give some thought to features such as hooks and built-in benches, which make any shower more convenient. Once again, the easier it is to use, the more it will be.

ABOVE A tapestry of branches makes up the walls of this rustic outdoor shower. Tucked into one corner of the porch, it takes advantage of the structure's stone floor and roof overhead.

RIGHT This concrete shower provides ample privacy without making you feel closed in. Concrete is a good material choice because it's one of the easiest to maintain.

A partial wall, fitted with a showerhead, provides just the right amount of privacy for rinsing off after a swim. Nearby, a similar set-up provides a place to hang towels—keeping them close but dry.

Facing an exterior wall, which accommodates the shower's hardware as well as a niche for soaps and shampoos, a curved half-wall made of bamboo is an uncomplicated way to cordon off a bathing area.

Located next to the pool, a tall concrete slab is fitted with a rainfall-style shower, making it convenient for swimmers to rinse off before and after a dip. Decorative knobs along one side keep towels close by, too.

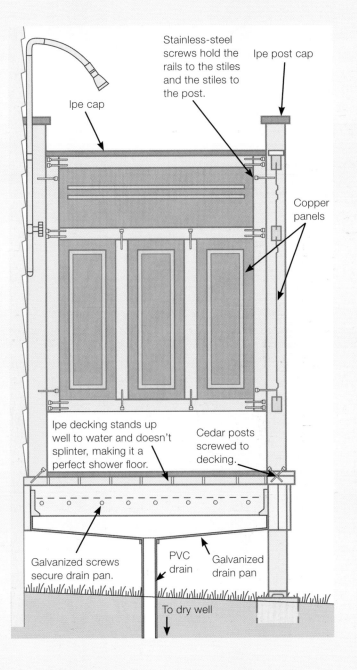

Ipe cap

Stainless-steel screws hold the rails to the stiles and the stiles to the post.

Ipe post cap

Copper panels

Ipe decking stands up well to water and doesn't splinter, making it a perfect shower floor.

Cedar posts screwed to decking.

Galvanized screws secure drain pan.

PVC drain

Galvanized drain pan

To dry well

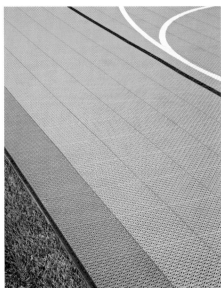

LEFT AND ABOVE For serious hoops fans or parents who want active kids, a backyard basketball court might be the answer. Because of prolonged sun exposure, opt for a surface with a UV coating to prevent discoloration.

play spaces

● ● ● TURNING YOUR BACKYARD INTO A PLACE FOR play will have great returns for your family life. Whether you install a sport court, a play structure, or an area for grass games, entertainment opportunities will be mere steps from your back door.

Sport courts can be tailored to any space. Volleyball, tennis, basketball, shuffleboard, paddle tennis, roller hockey, and skateboarding surfaces can be incorporated into the backyard in a wide variety of sizes. The court doesn't have to be the standard green, either; many companies offer a rainbow of colors. Consider custom options, too. You can personalize a surface with a logo or even a family crest.

Modern courts are often designed with a cushiony layer, which reduces the likelihood of injury. And look for one that comes in tile form. If an area becomes damaged, it can be replaced without having to tear up the entire surface.

ABOVE A respite from the sun on a hot tennis court, this thatched pavilion has enough room for a few spectators, along with a refrigerator for chilled water.

RIGHT A multipurpose court allows you to play a different sport almost every night. Here, a net is raised to tennis height, but it can be lifted even higher for a volleyball court. Remove the net completely and the space is ready for basketball.

create your own bocce court

Bocce, the Italian lawn-bowling game, can be played on the grass or the beach, but it's much more fun when you have a bona fide bocce court. To build one yourself, you'll need some construction experience—being able to understand, for example, the difference between the terms "plumb," "level," and "square." Plus, you'll want to consult local experts about drainage requirements in your area. The most common bocce court size is 10 feet by 60 feet, but 12 feet by 72 feet is great if you have the space to spare.

❶ REMOVE EXISTING LAWN with a shovel, sod cutter, or excavator. Dig the hole 5 inches deep. (You can make it more or less deep, depending on your drainage needs; the deeper it is, the less permeable it will be once it's filled in.)

❷ CUT 4-INCH BY 6-INCH LUMBER into 3-foot-6-inch posts. Mark spots for posts every 5 feet. Dig holes for the posts, about 2 feet 8 inches below ground level.

❸ FILL THE BOTTOM of the post holes with drain gravel (so that water won't become trapped and rot the posts). Secure posts with concrete, using about one bag of concrete per hole.

❹ ATTACH PERIMETER RAILS (3 by 10s) using ½-inch by 5½-inch lag screws with washers or outdoor #2 square head decking screws.

❺ LAY DOWN LANDSCAPE SEPARATION FABRIC to fit entire bottom surface of hole.

❻ YOU'RE GOING TO FILL with a total of 5 inches of base material, such as gravel or limestone (ask for commercial road base). Make sure the base is not "clean," as you want dirt to fill in the gaps between the individual stones. Fill 2 inches, and then compact it with a vibra plate or a plate compactor (both of which can be rented).

❼ LAY 3-INCH PERFORATED OR CORRUGATED DRAIN PIPES (with sleeves). Make sure the pipes are a minimum of 3 inches below the surface; closer to the top, and they could crack when someone walks on them. Add remaining 3 inches of base material, compacting again after the first 2.

❽ ADD 1.25 INCHES OF AN OYSTER-SHELL BLEND (such as Rain Country Blend, which includes a proprietary mix of oyster shell and other materials to make it more durable). This will put the surface above grade and aid drainage.

❾ MAINTAIN YOUR COURT with a 7-foot drag broom. An oyster-blend court should take 10 minutes to maintain.

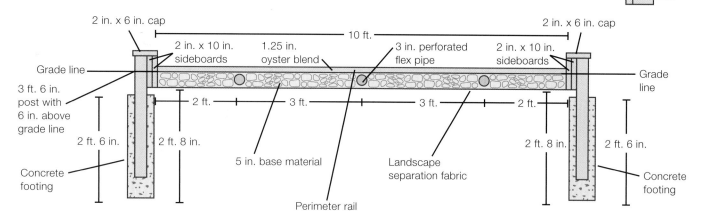

Corner Detail

2 in. x 6 in. cap

2 in. x 6 in. cap

10 ft.

2 in. x 10 in. sideboards

1.25 in. oyster blend

3 in. perforated flex pipe

2 in. x 10 in. sideboards

Grade line

Grade line

3 ft. 6 in. post with 6 in. above grade line

2 ft.

3 ft.

3 ft.

2 ft.

2 ft. 6 in.

2 ft. 8 in.

2 ft. 8 in.

2 ft. 6 in.

Concrete footing

5 in. base material

Landscape separation fabric

Concrete footing

Perimeter rail

ABOVE This concrete basketball court has an elevated seating section perfectly situated for spectators. When there's a crowd, the steps leading to it can double as bleachers.

BELOW A springy, water-pervious polypropylene surface, like the one used for this sports court, lets water seep through and minimizes the chance of injury, too.

RIGHT If Ping-Pong® is your game, look for a table that has corrosive-resistant surfaces and a weather-resistant net, so it can withstand even bad weather.

• yard games

A patch of lawn is like a blank canvas for many an outdoor game. There, you can set up something as structured as badminton or croquet, or as on-the-fly as backyard bowling, using nothing more than rubber balls and empty cereal boxes as "pins." Designed right, these games will disappear once victors have been declared, and the yard or garden can go back to its original state.

Surrounding a designated play area with colorful plantings makes for a beautiful space, and can provide great (and magical) hiding spots. Be sure to plan for game-related storage, whether it's a simple weather-proof chest or a freestanding shed. You want the games to be easy for the kids to access and, even more important, to put away.

FACING PAGE This flat, grassy area—just a few steps up from the nearby pool—provides a space that can be dedicated to all kinds of yard games. Its elevated nature also makes the overall landscape more appealing.

RIGHT At one end of this synthetic-turf putting surface, a catch net keeps golf balls from going astray. For these serious golfers, there's handy storage for putters and even a flag to indicate which way the wind s blowing.

LEFT An exciting way for kids to get from one side of the yard to the other, this pulley track works using gravity and body weight. Helmets are a must, though, as they can build up some speed.

ABOVE Pétanque, a French yard game played with metal balls, calls for a court made of gravel, but any loose-surface court that keeps the balls from rolling too far will suffice.

RIGHT A backyard putting green with real grass requires a lot of maintenance. Instead, consider synthetic options like this that don't need mowing or watering.

Short grass is the best surface for a game of croquet. A standard court is a 100-foot by 50-foot rectangle, but any size will do; simply define the boundaries with chalk, flags, or stakes.

m o r e   a b o u t ...
ARTIFICIAL LAWNS

becoming increasingly popular for its ease of care, artificial turf grass requires little water but looks surprisingly like the real thing. In fact, because it doesn't need to be watered, many drought-prone areas of the country offer rebates or tax breaks for homeowners who install artificial turf.

Since it's not real, this type of lawn of course requires no fertilizer (which, if not organic, can leach toxins into the water supply), no sprinklers, and—perhaps best of all—no mowing. You will still need to remove leaves and other debris, but overall, there's much less maintenance required.

There are some downsides, though. Some environmentalists say the petroleum products used to make artificial turf could allow chemicals to seep into groundwater. And it may produce more heat, which is worse for global warming. But keep in mind, too, that some companies, like NewGrass.com, are making their products with recycled plastic from water and soda bottles and are using compounds derived from soybeans, which—unlike petroleum—is a renewable resource.

• kids at play

The swingsets and play structures of today are more elaborate—and stimulating—than ever before. Colorful forts and castles can be built under large tree canopies, lidded sandboxes can be tucked into the landscape, and climbing walls can be added to other structures, such as jungle gyms.

The most successful designs incorporate the natural elements of your backyard, because they can arouse the imagination more than anything else. The beauty of a magnificent century-old oak is not lost on a child, so make it the focal point. Or if you're blessed with a large yard, add features that whisk children from one spot to another. If your home is on a hill, for example, install a slide so they can slip down from the top to the lower yard in no time at all. Adventure is the stuff of childhood.

In case of falls, the ground beneath any play area—like this one with a slide and climbing wall—should be soft. Materials such as recycled tires, wood chips, and even sand act as a great cushion.

ABOVE Several trees work together to anchor this elaborate design, the swinging bridges connecting one to another. And because it's somewhat camouflaged, it's even more fun for creative minds.

LEFT A small shed can be transformed into a playhouse for the younger set. Appoint it with a pint-size picnic table and small-scale furnishings that work both indoors and out.

ABOVE A fairytale seemingly materializes in this whimsical playhouse, featuring—among other things—a slide and climbing wall. Building the play structure around an existing tree makes it even more of an adventure.

RIGHT "Fort Rice" is more than a tree house; it's an outdoor play paradise. The slide deposits kids directly into a sandbox, which is both a soft landing surface and a new spot to play.

Dedicating a section of the yard to the kids' equipment keeps them corralled and gives the adults a space of their own. Provide a variety of play options so they can rotate among them without getting bored.

BELOW This souped-up swing set includes a climbing wall and rope, but takes up the same amount of space as a more conventional design.

LEFT AND BELOW This L-shaped play structure has so many entry and exit points, it creates infinite places to hide and play. And no space is wasted: The bridge in the center also supports a pair of swings.

backyard buildings

● ● ●

FOR SOME, THE ALLURE OF THE BACKYARD FORT IS NOT JUST A childhood fixation; it's a lifelong attraction. And today's backyard structures can satisfy that need, allowing you to commune with nature while escaping the minutiae of daily life.

A backyard building can also serve a more utilitarian purpose, like accommodating friends and family who come to visit for the weekend. Or housing a desk and workspace for writing that great American novel. Or for storing tools needed for the garden and yard. It could be a place for entertainment, sports, dining, or parties; there are as many options as you can imagine—and possibly some you can't.

First, think about how you plan to use the space. Will it function as a leisurely retreat? Or will you be more pragmatic, using the extra square footage for a home office?

Then research design options—you can go online and look in plan books for information about cottages, sheds, and other outbuildings. Next, hire a carpenter or build it yourself. You might even consult an architect to help you with a customized space. Remember, too, that there are a variety of attractive pre-fab options on the market today; all that's needed is assembly.

Backyard structures can be practical or more decorative. This gazebo is both, offering a spot for socializing and a striking tower-like silhouette that echoes that of the surrounding flowers.

places for relaxation

●●● OUR HOMES TEND TO BE FILLED WITH ROOMS that are associated with tasks or goals. We cook in the kitchen and work in the office. But sometimes we crave a spot with no designated purpose, one with no attendant to-do lists. Using a small cottage or cabin as a getaway puts the backyard to work for therapeutic ends. Whether you're looking for a place to practice yoga or simply enjoy the serenity of nature, you don't need a lot of acreage to get the results you want.

A number of companies offer cabin kits that are ideal for relaxation. They can be assembled by any DIYer, which makes them affordable and attainable for many people who otherwise never dreamed of having a backyard outbuilding. And these spaces offer something intangible, too: A renewal of spirit that is hard to replicate in a busy household.

RIGHT Engulfed by a profusion of blooms as they clamber up a metal trellis, this garden room is defined by open walls and a ceiling but still maintains a connection with the rest of the yard.

FACING PAGE Paver stepping stones lead to this pavilion, a quiet retreat that spans a small pond stocked with goldfish. The simple, understated furnishings within further enhance the feeling of serenity.

LEFT A small pre-fab building turns this once-nondescript backyard into a little slice of paradise. Sliding glass doors span the front of the structure, filling it with warmth and light.

ABOVE AND RIGHT This two-car garage was transformed into a warm and welcoming pool house. The plush sofas and chairs, a beachy color scheme, and grasscloth-covered walls give the space a bright, airy disposition.

FACING PAGE If you're a fan of yoga, create a wood pad for the purpose of practicing your sport. Surrounding it with a lush garden makes it all the easier to get into the right state of mind.

more about...
PRE-FAB STRUCTURES

ever increasing in popularity, pre-fab outbuildings come in many forms—from cottages and yurts to sheds and studios. While they aren't inexpensive, they will cost you less than having one designed and built from scratch.

A typical pre-fab structure is first built in a factory, then assembled on your property—either by the company or by yourself. Many, in fact, can be put together by a couple of people in a weekend.

Before purchasing a pre-fab building, find out what is and is not included. For example, be sure it's pre-wired for electricity, and will accommodate plumbing, too. Consider the quality of the windows, doors, and insulation, so you'll know how efficiently it can be heated and cooled. And keep in mind that some pre-fab models don't come with finished flooring, so you'll have to factor that into your budget.

RIGHT A curved path leading to this garden structure gives it the aura of a true destination. Outfitted with a pro-level stove and proper ventilation, this building can be used to make meals year-round.

FACING PAGE A pavilion is home to an outdoor kitchen that includes a wood-fired pizza oven and plenty of dining space. The slatted roof lets in plenty of sunlight and keeps the air circulating, too.

Because there are supportive posts only on one side, a cantilevered pergola is a real space-saver, leaving more room for the entertaining area below.

pavilions, pergolas, and gazebos

● ● ● ALL RIGHT AT HOME IN THE BACKYARD, pavilions, pergolas, and gazebos are similar in structure. A gazebo is simply a smaller version of a pavilion; both typically have solid roofs with at least partially open sides. Pergolas, on the other hand, tend to have latticed or slatted roofs, allowing the light—and rain—to come through. In colder climes, you can put a sheet of acrylic over the open roof, allowing in sunlight but keeping out the wind.

Before adding one of these structures to your backyard, check on local building codes. Even if you don't think of yours as a "building" per se, there may be governed requirements for its size, height, and materials.

RIGHT A modern take on a pergola involves walls of shuttered doors and windows. Over the dining table, a domed roof delineates the eating area while providing protection from the elements.

LEFT A wooden pergola, allowed to weather to a silvery gray, features built-in benches on either side, allowing you to take in the beauty of the surrounding garden.

Pendulous wisteria pokes through the openings in a trellis, filling the space with a wonderful fragrance and a stunning purple color when the flowers bloom come spring.

planning for a gazebo

The characteristics of each yard, and each homeowner, call for a different gazebo. To determine what will best suit your needs, take these preliminary steps:

❶ ASK YOURSELF if you want your gazebo to stand out or blend in. For example, to hide a hulking hot tub, paint the structure a dark color like black or dark green and place it in an inconspicuous corner of the yard. On the other hand, if you want the gazebo to be a focal point, make it a light color that stands out against the backdrop of greenery and create a path that leads the eye right to it. Treat it like the decorative element that it is. That means even considering how it will look when you're peering at it from inside the house.

❷ DO SOME RESEARCH. Study gazebo styles that are in keeping with the era and architecture of your home to get a sense of what is appropriate. Different eras and types of homes pair with different gazebo designs, and you want them to be congruous.

❸ CONSIDER CLIMATE. If you experience cold winters in your area and plan to use the gazebo year-round—with a spa, for example—be sure to include windows, walls, doors, and heating in your plan.

❹ LOOK INTO GAZEBO KITS. Today's kits are easy to construct and cost less than built-from-scratch structures. And they can be customized by simply adding or omitting features such as panels and doors.

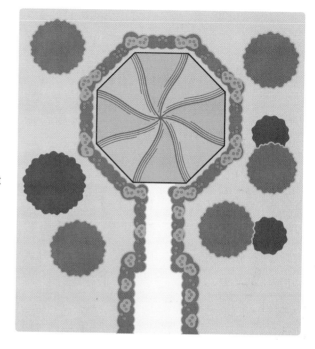

LEFT The materials in this contemporary pavilion take a layered approach, each one outstanding in its own right. A concrete fireplace wall forms the foundation, topped with stacked-stone and a ribbed metal roof.

RIGHT AND FACING PAGE
This square stucco pavilion feels like an exclusive nook. Lined with comfy seating in a festive red, the structure also features strings of lights hanging from the ceiling, adding to the party atmosphere.

BELOW Small trellises can be arranged to create the border of a garden space. Bursting with blooms, these team up with benches to create several quiet sitting spots.

offices and studios

● ● ● MANY A HOME OFFICE SHARES ITS SPACE WITH a craft room, guest room, or even kitchen. Multipurpose rooms like this can be practical, but perhaps not the most efficient. Enter: the backyard office. By erecting an outdoor building that will serve as a dedicated office or studio, you can free up space inside and work more effectively, too.

Likewise, if you work from home, a backyard office is an especially appealing option, as the chaos of home life can sometimes prohibit productivity. But it still gives you an enviable commute (just minutes, if not seconds).

Keep the structure close to the main house, giving you easy access to the kitchen, bathroom, and other essentials. But at the same time, make sure it feels far enough away that you're able to actually get something accomplished. For the best of both, tuck it into a corner of the yard or surround it with plantings to provide an extra element of seclusion.

ABOVE This 65-square-foot pre-fab structure makes the most of its limited space. There's a desk, sleeping loft, and even two closets—just enough for an office or studio.

FACING PAGE A grown-up version of a tree house, this studio gets plenty of light through the windows but is shaded at the same time by the canopy of branches above.

ABOVE Though sleek and modern, this office fits right into the woodsy setting. Thanks to the windows that extend all the way to the peaked roof, light from within shines like a beacon.

FACING PAGE AND LEFT Once a storage shed, this building was transformed into a painter's studio that now has an inspiring view of the gardens. The adjoining deck allows the artist-in-residence to pull an easel outside on sunny days.

BELOW This contemporary pre-fab cabin is modern enough for urban environs, but could just as well fit in the country. Because of the almost-10-foot ceiling and the line of windows, it feels deceptively spacious inside.

ABOVE Suitable for storing tools or as a small art studio, this 10-foot by 12-foot pre-fab shed arrives pre-painted. You can choose how to configure it, opting for the door in one of many locations.

BELOW Outbuildings once intended for live-in gardeners can be turned into studios or workshops. A benefit? The placement, typically at one end of the garden, presents a wonderful view.

An outdoor studio or office can reflect your
personality, just like a primary residence. Here,
a cottage-style space proves inspiring for an
avid gardener.

sheds

●●● ON THE SURFACE, A SHED SEEMS PRETTY STRAIGHT-forward: It's a place to keep your tools and yard equipment. What many people don't realize, though, is how many design choices there are. Just because a shed is practical doesn't mean it can't be beautiful, from outside or in. Rooflines can vary from gable and gambrel to saltbox and lean-to, while colors can be even more vibrant than you'd dare use on your home. It's a prime opportunity to let your personality show through. To make it even more appealing, include at least one window, preferably with a view of the garden itself so you can marvel at the fruits of your labor.

In any shed, however, function should be the top priority. Shelves, cabinets, and all manner of storage can organize the interior to the nth degree. The key is to make use of all surfaces, even the walls. Instead of throwing larger tools into tangled piles, for instance, hang them from a pegboard or hooks.

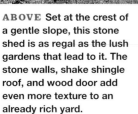

ABOVE Set at the crest of a gentle slope, this stone shed is as regal as the lush gardens that lead to it. The stone walls, shake shingle roof, and wood door add even more texture to an already rich yard.

RIGHT Even the smallest shed can provide the jolt of color a backyard needs. This bright coral, with a green door, introduces a happy vibe.

A quaint cottagey shed can be designed to mimic the house, but with practical features as well—such as double doors that allow for easy maneuvering of large yard equipment like a lawnmower.

make a rustic tool holder

by John C. Fech

❶ FIND AN OLD RAKE with a broken handle.

❷ CUT OFF THE HANDLE, turn the rake upside down, and nail it in place on a shed or garage wall with the tines facing outward.

❸ ON THE TINES, hang large tools with D-shaped handles as well as smaller tools such as trowels and hand weeders.

This project originally appeared in Fine Gardening, *No. 40*

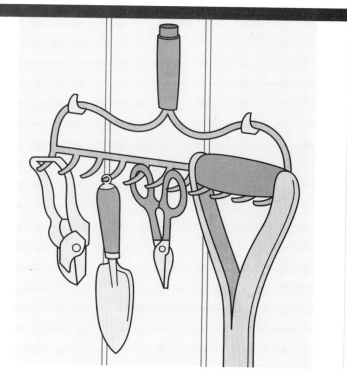

gallery

greenhouses

For the avid gardener, a greenhouse offers a space to tinker with plants throughout the year, no matter the weather. But even for the casual hobbyist, a greenhouse can incorporate both a workspace and a living-relaxing area, allowing you to enjoy gardening on an entirely new level.

If you're just starting out, a lean-to greenhouse is a good place to begin. It's positioned against the house and is usually small, with just one or two rows of plant benches. And its proximity to the house gives you easy access to electricity and water hookups.

When buying a greenhouse, find out if the purchase price includes installation. Because heating and cooling systems are typically necessary, putting one up is a project often best left to the pros.

When siting the greenhouse, look for a spot that gets plenty of light—a minimum of five hours a day during the winter months. The best place is usually on the south or southeast side of the house; the north side tends to be too light-deprived for this type of structure.

1 A roll shade controls the sunlight allowed into this greenhouse.

2 This green-house has a floor that allows drainage.

3 Side-by-side tables provide ample workspace

4 This greenhouse doubles as a backyard escape.

5 A greenhouse establishes a link between two brick structures.

6 Staggered shelving accommodates pots of various sizes.

2

1

3

4

5

6

POTTING TABLES

e ven without a full-fledged shed or greenhouse, you can have a functional, usable outdoor workspace. The piece may be nothing more than a sink, some shelves, and a simple work surface but if you're looking for a potting table, what more do you need?

When choosing a potting table, look for one with ample storage space, as well as a generous work surface. Built-in drawers, cubbies, and shelves make it easy to keep tools at hand so that the task of potting plants or arranging flowers is orderly. Also look for materials that are weather resistant, so that they can survive being outside, without requiring much maintenance. The work station shouldn't make more work for you; it should make the work you already have easier.

1

2

1 Sinks can be utilitarian and good-looking, too. This embossed-concrete version—its faucet mounted above—stands out prominently against the darker brick wall.

2 Stacks of terra-cotta pots have a countrified beauty; they're organized yet still rustic. The open walls and roof bring some of the garden even closer, as eager vines make their way up and across.

3 Your garden tools don't have to be hidden away. In fact, this red rake hung on the door wakes up the workstation with a dose of color; plus, making it easy to grab means you won't put off doing so.

4 A flagstone countertop, chicken-wire cabinet doors, and wainscoting set a lovely scene in which to get some work done. Even the fixture adds to the ambience, while providing direct light for various tasks.

resources

DESIGNERS AND ARCHITECTS:

Abramson Teiger Architects
8924 Lindblade Street
Culver City, CA 90232
310-838-8998
www.abramsonteiger.com

Ania Lejman Design Company
1201 Montana Avenue, Suite 201
Santa Monica, CA 90403
310-578-8488
www.aldco.com

**ARTECHO Architecture and
Landscape Architecture/
Pamela Palmer**
1639 Electric Avenue, Suite A
Venice, CA 90291
310-399-4794
www.artecho.com

Atlas Design
608 Ocampo Drive
Pacific Palisades, CA 90272
atlas.design@mac.com

Barbara Butler Artist/Builder Inc.
325 South Maple Avenue, #37
South San Francisco, CA 94080
415-864-6840
www.barbarabutler.com

Boccemon
705 Carolina Street
Bellingham, WA 98225
360-224-2909
www.boccemon.com

Burdge & Associates Architects
21235 Pacific Coast Highway
Malibu, CA 90265
office@buaia.com
www.buaia.com

Dewing and Schmid Architects
30 Monument Square, Suite 200B
Concord, MA 01742
978-371-7500
280 Elm Street and South Dartmouth,
MA 02748
508-999-0440
www.dsarch.com

Houston/Tyner Architects
13444 Bali Way
Marina Del Rey, CA 90292
houstontyner@earthlink.net

Jonny Appleseed Landscape Inc.
PO Box 7010
Beverly Hills, CA 90212
310-419-7660
www.jonnyappleseed.net

Katie Moss Landscape Design
West Los Angeles, CA
310-569-5333
www.katiemoss.com

Lenkin Design
1112 Lagunita Road
Pasadena, CA 91105
626-441-6655
www.LenkinDesign.com

Maraya Droney Design
1712 Ladera Road
Ojai, CA 93023
805-646-6673
www.maraya.com

Ramirez Design Inc.
428 Alta Avenue
Santa Monica, CA 90402
310-395-2192
www.ramirezstudio.com

Rhino Sports/Dream Courts
30941 Agoura Road, Suite 126
Westlake Village, CA 91361
818-874-1477
www.labackyardcourts.com

Stout Landscape Design
12405 Venice Boulevard, #352
Los Angeles, CA 90066
310-876-1018
www.stoutlandscape.com

PRODUCT SOURCES:

Capel Rugs
800-382-6574
www.capelrugs.com
(outdoor rugs)

Fermob
706-216-6605
www.fermobUSA.com
(patio and garden seating)

La Puerta Originals
4523 State Road, Highway 14
Santa Fe, NM 87508
(505) 984-8164
www.lapuertaoriginals.com
(gates and fences)

Maku Furniture
760-930-0081
www.makufurniture.com
(sustainable patio and garden furniture)

Metro Shed
(310) 295-0072
www.metroshed.com
(prefab outbuildings)

Modern Shed
(206) 524-1188
www.modern-shed.com
(prefab outbuildings)

Private Garden Greenhouse Systems
A Division of Hampden Structural
Systems
36 Commercial Drive
PO Box 600
Hampden, MA 01036
413-566-0277
www.private-garden.com
(greenhouses)

Sunbrella
336-221-2211
www.Sunbrella.com
(weather- and sun-resistant fabrics)

Tumbleweed Tiny House Company
web@tumbleweedhouses.com
www.tumbleweedhouses.com
(prefab outbuildings)

Walpole Woodworkers
800-343-6948
www.walpolewoodworkers.com
(outdoor structures)

ORGANIZATIONS:

The American Institute of Architects
202-626-7300
www.aia.org

**Association of Pool and Spa
Professionals**
703-838-0083
www.apsp.org

**Association of Professional
Landscape Designers**
717-238-9780
www.apld.org

**American Society of Landscape
Architects**
202-898-2444
www.asla.org

National Spa & Pool Institute
703-838-0083
www.nspi.org

United States Croquet Association
561-478-0760
www.croquetamerica.com

photo credits

p.ii: Photo © Rob Karosis, Design: Charles C Hugo Landscape Design LLC
p.v: Photo © Jack Coyier Photography, Design: ARTECHO Architecture and Landscape Architecture/Pamela Palmer, www.artecho.com
p.vi: (1) Photo © Philip Beaurline; (2) Photo © Jack Coyier Photography, Design: ARTECHO Architecture and Landscape Architecture/Pamela Palmer, www.artecho.com; (3) Photo © Philip Beaurline; (4) Photo © Mark Lohman; (5) Photo © Philip Beaurline;
p. 1: Photo © Jack Coyier Photography, Design: Jon Goldstein of Jonny Appleseed Landscape, Inc., www.jonnyappleseed.net
p. 2: (left) Photo © Mali Azima; (right) Photo © Jack Coyier Photography, Design: ARTECHO Architecture and Landscape Architecture/Pamela Palmer, www.artecho.com
p. 3: Photo © Mark Lohman, Design: Ramirez Design Inc.

CHAPTER 1

p. 4: Photo © Philip Beaurline
p. 5: (top to bottom) Photo © Mark Lohman; Photo © Brian Vanden Brink, Design: Whitten Architects; Photo © Eric Roth; Photo © Brian Vanden Brink, Design: Stephen Blatt Architects
p. 6: Photo © Eric Roth
p. 7: Photo © Mark Lohman
p. 8: Photo © Philip Beaurline; Design: Robert Paxton; Dalgleish, Gilpin & Paxton
p. 9: Photos © Mark Lohman
p. 10: (top) Photo © Brian Vanden Brink, Design: Whitten Architects; (bottom) Photo © Philip Beaurline, Design: Robert Gray; Shank & Gray Architects
p. 11: (top) Photo © Mark Lohman, Design: Ramirez Design, Inc.; (bottom left) Photo © Philip Beaurline; (bottom right) Photo © Mark Lohman, Design: Ramirez Design, Inc.
p. 12: Photo © Eric Roth
p. 13: (top) Photo © Eric Roth; (bottom) Photo © Mark Lohman, Design: Kyser Interiors
p.14: Photo © Mark Lohman, Design: Trent Hultgren
p. 15 (top) Photo © Jennifer Cheung and Steven Nilsson, Design: Carolyn Watson; (bottom) Photo © Rob Karosis, Design: Charles C. Hugo Landscape Design, LLC
p. 16: (top) Photo © Jack Coyier Photography, Design: Gary Mason, Sanctuary Landscape Design; (bottom) Photo © Philip Beaurline, Design: Doug Gilpin; Dalgleish, Gilpin & Paxton
p. 17: Photo © Jennifer Cheung and Steven Nilsson, Design: Heather Lenkin of www.lenkindesign.com
p. 18: (left) Photo © Rob Karosis, Design: Charles C. Hugo Landscape Design, LLC;
p. 19: Photo © Jennifer Cheung and Steven Nilsson, Design: Heather Lenkin of www.lenkindesign.com
p. 20: Photo © Mark Lohman, Design: Ramirez Design Inc.
p. 21: (left) Photo © Brian Vanden Brink, Design: Hutker Architects; Horiuchi & Solien, Landscape Architecture, (right) Photo © Jennifer Cheung and Steven Nilsson, Design: Rick Button
p. 22: Photo © Jennifer Cheung and Steven Nilsson, Design: Rick Button
p. 23: (left) Photo © Jennifer Cheung and Steven Nilsson, (right) Photo © Jennifer Cheung and Steven Nilsson, Design: Heather Lenkin of www.lenkindesign.com,
p. 24: Photo © Jack Coyier Photography, Design: Ania Lejman, www.aldco.com
p. 25: Photo © Mark Lohman, Design: Kathryne Designs
p. 26: (top) Photo © Mark Lohman, Design: Tom Stout Landscape; (bottom) Photo © Mark Lohman, Design: Houston/Tyner Architects, Brad Jenson Construction, and Kathryne Designs
p. 27: Photo © Jack Coyier Photography, Design: John Bilac, Picture Perfect Construction (installation), www.pictureperfectconstruction.com
p. 28: (top) Photo © Mark Lohman; (bottom) Photo © Philip Beaurline
p. 29: (left) Photo © Brian Vanden Brink, Design: Polhemus Savery DaSilva Architects Builders; (right) Photo © Mark Lohman, Design: Trent Hultgren
p. 30: Photo © Brian Vanden Brink, Design: Elliott Elliott Norelius Architecture
p. 31: Photo © Brian Vanden Brink, Design: Stephen Blatt Architects
p. 32: Photo © Eric Roth, Design: www.greencos.com
p. 33: Photo © Mark Lohman
p.34: Photo © Jack Coyier Photography, Design: Jon Goldstein of Jonny Appleseed Landscape, Inc., www.jonnyappleseed.net
p.35: (top) Photo © Philip Beaurline; (bottom) Photo © Jennifer Cheung and Steven Nilsson, Design: Heather Lenkin of www.lenkindesign.com
p. 36: (left) Photo © Mark Lohman, Design: Maraya Droney Design, Marlene Ayerle, and Brian Lehrman; (right) Photo © Jennifer Cheung and Steven Nilsson, Design: Heather Lenkin of www.lenkindesign.com
p. 37: (top left) Photo © Jack Coyier Photography, Design: Ania Lejman, www.aldco.com
(top right) Photo © Jack Coyier Photography, Design: Jon Goldstein of Jonny Appleseed Landscape, Inc., www.jonnyappleseed.net
(bottom left) Photo © Mark Lohman, Design: Burdge & Assoc.; (bottom right) Photo © Mark Lohman, Design: Tom Stout Landscape Design and Abramson Teiger Architects
p. 38: Photo © Eric Roth, Design: www.greencos.com
p. 39: (left) Photo © Eric Roth; (right) Photo © Jennifer Cheung and Steven Nilsson
p. 40: Photo © Philip Beaurline, Design: Robert Paxton; Dalgleish, Gilpin & Paxton
p. 41: (top) Photo © Mali Azima; (bottom) Photo © Jennifer Cheung and Steven Nilsson, Design: Sandy Koepke
p. 42: Photo © Jennifer Cheung and Steven Nilsson, Design: Heather Lenkin of www.lenkindesign.com
p. 43: Photo © Mali Azima, Design: Landscape design by RichardAndersonLA.com

CHAPTER 2

p. 44: Photo © Jack Coyier Photography, Design: ARTECHO Architecture and Landscape Architecture/Pamela Palmer, www.artecho.com
p. 45: (top to bottom) Photo © Mali Azima; Photo © Mali Azima; Photo © Jack Coyier Photography, Design: ARTECHO Architecture and Landscape Architecture/ Pamela Palmer, www.artecho.com; Photo © Mark Lohman, Design: Houston/Tyner Architects, Brad Jenson Construction, and Kathryne Designs
p. 46 :(top) Photo © Jack Coyier Photography, Design: Jon Goldstein of Jonny Appleseed Landscape, Inc., www.jonnyappleseed.net; (bottom) Photo © Mark Lohman, Design: Atlas Design and Ray Kinner Builders
p. 47: Photo © Mark Lohman, Design: Ramirez Design, Inc.
p. 48: Photo © Mark Lohman, Design: Ramirez Design, Inc.
p. 49: (top) Photo © Jack Coyier Photography, Design: Christopher Mercier, www.ferstudio.com (bottom left) Photo © Mark Lohman, Design: Tom Stout Landscape, Anthony Eckelberry Architect, and Linda Spiegel, Design (bottom right) Photo © Jennifer Cheung and Steven Nilsson, Design: Heather Lenkin of www.lenkindesign.com
p. 50: (top) Photo © Jack Coyier Photography, Design: Ania Lejman, www.aldco.com (bottom) Rob Karosis, Design: Charles C. Hugo Landscape Design, LLC
p. 52: (top) Photo © Mark Lohman); (bottom) Photo © Mark Lohman, Design: Maraya Droney Design, Marlene Ayerle and Brian Lehrman
p. 53: Photo © Mali Azima, Design: Furniture, pillows and rug by LaneVenture
p. 54: Photos © Jack Coyier Photography, Design: Katie Moss Landscape Design, www.katiemoss.com
p. 56: (left) Photo © Mark Lohman; (right) Photo © Mark Lohman, Design: Houston/Tyner Architects, Brad Jenson Construction, and Kathryne Designs
p. 57: Photo © Mark Lohman, Design: Don & Jackie McCune Design, Inc.
p. 58:
(1) Photo © Mark Lohman, Design: Maraya Droney Design, Marlene Ayerle, and Brian Lehrman
(2) Photo © Mark Lohman, Design: Tom Stout Landscape
(3) Photo © Mark Lohman, Design: Burdge & Assoc.
p. 59: Photo © Mark Lohman, Design: Ramirez Design, Inc.
p. 60: Photo © Mark Lohman
p. 61: Photos © Mark Lohman
p. 62: (left) Photo © Mark Lohman, Design: Don & Jackie McCune Design, Inc.; (right) Photo © Mark Lohman, Design: Tom Stout Landscape, Anthony Eckelberry Architect, and Linda Spiegel Design
p. 63: (top) Photo © Mark Lohman, Design: Don & Jackie McCune Design, Inc.; (bottom) Photo © Mark Lohman, Design: Houston/Tyner Architects, Brad Jenson Construction, and Kathryne Designs
p. 64: Photo © Jennifer Cheung and Steven Nilsson, Design: Heather Lenkin of www.lenkindesign.com
p.65: Photo © Jack Coyier Photography, Design: John Bilac, Picture Perfect Construction (installation), www.pictureperfectconstruction.com
p. 66: Photo © Mark Lohman
p. 67: (top left) Photo © Mark Lohman, Design: Don & Jackie McCune Design, Inc.; (bottom left) Photo © Mark Lohman, Design: Burdge & Assoc.; (bottom right) Photo © Mark Lohman, Design: Maraya Droney Design, Marlene Ayerle and Brian Lehrman
p.68: Photo © Mark Lohman, Design: Tom Stout Landscape
p. 69: (top) Photo © Jack Coyier Photography, Design: Jon Goldstein of Jonny Appleseed Landscape, Inc., www.jonnyappleseed.net; (bottom) Photo © Mark Lohman, Design: Tom Stout Landscape, Anthony Eckelberry Architect, and Linda Spiegel Design
p. 70: (left) Photo © Mali Azima, Design: Brian Patrick Flynn; (right) Photo © Brian Vanden Brink, Design: Weatherend Estate Furniture
p. 71: Photos © Jennifer Cheung and Steven Nilsson and Design: Heather Lenkin of www.lenkindesign.com
p. 72: (top) Photo © Jennifer Cheung and Steven Nilsson, Design: Sandy Koepke (bottom) Photo © Mali Azima
p. 73: (top) Photo © Jennifer Cheung and Steven Nilsson Design: Sandy Koepke; (bottom) Photo © Mali Azima
p. 74: Photo © Mark Lohman, Design: Houston/Tyner Architects, Brad Jenson Construction, and Kathryne Designs
p. 75: Photo © Mark Lohman, Design: Tom Stout Landscape
p. 76: Photo © Mark Lohman, Design: Burdge & Assoc.
p. 77: Photo © Mark Lohman, Design: Maraya Droney Design, Marlene Ayerle, and Brian Lehrman
p. 78: Photo © Mark Lohman, Design: Ramirez Design, Inc.
p. 79: (top) Photo © Jack Coyier Photography, Design: Ania Lejman, www.aldco.com; (bottom) Jennifer Cheung and Steven Nilsson Design: Gabriela Yariv
p. 80: (top) Photo © Jack Coyier Photography, Design: ARTECHO Architecture and Landscape Architecture/ Pamela Palmer, www.artecho.com; (bottom) Photo © Mark Lohman, Design: Tom Stout Landscape, Anthony Eckelberry Architect, and Linda Spiegel Design
p. 81: Photo © Mali Azima
p. 82: Photo © Jack Coyier Photography, Design: Ania Lejman, www.aldco.com
p. 83: (top) Photo © Jack Coyier Photography, Design: ARTECHO Architecture and Landscape Architecture/ Pamela Palmer, www.artecho.com; (bottom) Photo © Jack Coyier Photography, Design: Jon Goldstein of Jonny Appleseed Landscape, Inc., www.jonnyappleseed.net
p. 84: Photo © Jennifer Cheung and Steven Nilsson
p. 85: Photo © Jack Coyier Photography, Design: Katie Moss Landscape Design, www.katiemoss.com
p. 86: (left) Photo © Jennifer Cheung and Steven Nilsson, Design: Heather Lenkin of www.lenkindesign.com; (right) Photo © Mark Lohman, Design: Burdge & Assoc.
p. 87: Photo © Scott Phillips
p. 88: (top) Photo © Mark Lohman, Design: Tom Stout Landscape; (bottom) Photo © Mark Lohman, Design: Atlas Design and Ray Kinner Builders
p. 89: Photo © Jennifer Cheung and Steven Nilsson, Design: Heather Lenkin of www.lenkindesign.com
p. 90: (left) Photo © Eric Roth, Design: www.greencos.com; (right) Photo © Mark Lohman, Design: Palm Design Group
p. 91: Photo © Jennifer w and Steven Nilsson, Design: Carolyn Watson
p. 92: Photos © Jack Coyier Photography, Design: Christopher Mercier, www.ferstudio.com
p. 93: Photo © Jack Coyier Photography, Design: Gary Mason, Sanctuary Landscape Design
p. 94: (top) Photo © Jennifer Cheung and Steven Nilsson; (bottom) Photo © Mark Lohman
p. 95: Photo © Jack Coyier Photography, Design: ARTECHO Architecture and Landscape Architecture/Pamela Palmer, www.artecho.com
p. 96: Photo © Mark Lohman, Design: Maraya Droney Design, Marlene Ayerle, and Brian Lehrman
p. 97: (top) Photo © Mark Lohman, Design: Tom Stout Landscape, Anthony Eckelberry Architect, and Linda Spiegel Design); (bottom) Photo © Mark Lohman, Design: Houston/Tyner Architects, Brad Jenson Construction, and Kathryne Designs

CHAPTER 3

p. 98: Photo © Philip Beaurline
p. 99: (top to bottom) Photo © Jennifer Cheung and Steven Nilsson, Design: Heather Lenkin of www.lenkindesign.com; Photo © Jennifer Cheung and Steven Nilsson, Design: Heather Lenkin of www.lenkindesign.com; Photo © Mark Lohman; Photo © Jennifer Cheung and Steven Nilsson, Design: Gabriela Yariv
p. 100: Photo © Mali Azima
p. 101: (top) Photo © Mali Azima, Design: Landscape design by Bill Hudgins of Lush Life; furniture, pillows, and throw by LaneVenture; (bottom) Photo © Jack Coyier Photography, Design: John Bilac, Picture Perfect Construction (installation), www.pictureperfectconstruction.com
p. 102: (top) Photo © Mali Azima; (bottom) Photo © Brian Vanden Brink
p. 103: Photo © Mark Lohman
p. 104: Photo © Mark Lohman

p. 105: (top) Photo © Rob Karosis, Design: Charles C Hugo Landscape Design LLC; (bottom) Photo © Mark Lohman

p. 106: Photos © Jack Coyier Photography, Design: Ania Lejman, www.aldco.com

p. 107: Photo © Jennifer Cheung and Steven Nilsson, Design: Heather Lenkin of www.lenkindesign.com

p. 108: Photo © Jennifer Cheung and Steven Nilsson, Design: Heather Lenkin of www.lenkindesign.com

p. 109: (top) Photo © Mark Lohman, Design: Burdge & Assoc.; (bottom) Photo © Mark Lohman, Design: Tom Stout Landscape

p. 110: Photo © Jennifer Cheung and Steven Nilsson, Design: Rick Button

p. 111: (top) Photo © Jack Coyier Photography, Design: Ania Lejman, www.aldco.com; (bottom) Photo © Jennifer Cheung and Steven Nilsson, Design: Heather Lenkin of www.lenkindesign.com

p. 112: Photo © Mark Lohman

p. 113: Photos © Jennifer Cheung and Steven Nilsson, Design: Heather Lenkin of www.lenkindesign.com

p. 114: (left) Photo © Jack Coyier Photography, Design: Ania Lejman, www.aldco.com; (top right) Photo © Mali Azima, Design: John Byrd Garden Design; (bottom right) Photo © Jack Coyier Photography, Design: ARTECHO Architecture and Landscape Architecture/Pamela Palmer, www.artecho.com

p. 115: (top) Photo © Jennifer Cheung and Steven Nilsson, Design: Heather Lenkin of www.lenkindesign.com; (bottom left) Photo © Mark Lohman Design:Tom Stout Landscape; (bottom right) Photo © Jack Coyier Photography, Design: Jon Goldstein of Jonny Appleseed Landscape, Inc., www.jonnyappleseed.net

p. 116: (top) Photo © Brian Vanden Brink; (bottom) Photo © Jennifer Cheung and Steven Nilsson

p. 117: Photo © Jack Coyier Photography, Design: Ania Lejman, www.aldco.com

p. 118: Photo © Jennifer Cheung and Steven Nilsson, Design: Heather Lenkin of www.lenkindesign.com

p. 119: (top left) Photo © Philip Beaurline; (top right) Photo © Jennifer Cheung and Steven Nilsson, Design: Rick Button; (bottom) Courtesy of La Puerta

p. 120: (top) Photo © Brian Vanden Brink, Design:Ron Forest Fences; (bottom) Photo © Mark Lohman

p. 121: Photo © Brian Vanden Brink, Design: Horiuchi & Solien, Landscape Architecture

p. 122: Photo © Mali Azima, Design: David McMullin

p. 123: Photos © Photos Mark Lohman, Design:Tom Stout Landscape

p. 124: Photo © Brian Vanden Brink

p. 125: (top) Photo © Brian Vanden Brink; (bottom) Photo © Mark Lohman

p. 126: Photos © Jennifer Cheung and Steven Nilsson, Design: Heather Lenkin of www.lenkindesign.com;

p. 127: (top) Photo © Jennifer Cheung and Steven Nilsson, Design: Gabriela Yariv (bottom) Photo © Mali Azima

p. 128: Photo © Jennifer Cheung and Steven Nilsson, Design: Heather Lenkin of www.lenkindesign.com; (bottom left) Photo © Mali Azima

p. 129: (top left) Photo © Mali Azima; (top right) Photo © Jennifer Cheung and Steven Nilsson, Design: Heather Lenkin of www.lenkindesign.com; (bottom) Photo © Jennifer Cheung and Steven Nilsson, Design: Sandy Koepke

p. 130: (left) Photo © Mark Lohman, Design: Tom Stout Landscape; (top right) Photo © Jack Coyier Photography, Design: ARTECHO Architecture and Landscape Architecture/Pamela Palmer, www.artecho.com; (bottom) Photo © Jack Coyier Photography, Design: Ania Lejman, www.aldco.com

p. 131: (top) Photo © Jennifer Cheung and Steven Nilsson, Design: Gabriela Yariv; (bottom right) Photo © Jennifer Cheung and Steven Nilsson, Design: Heather Lenkin of www.lenkindesign.com

p. 132: Photo © Philip Beaurline

p. 133: Photos © Jennifer Cheung and Steven Nilsson, Design: Heather Lenkin of www.lenkindesign.com

p. 134: Photo © Eric Roth

p. 135: Photos © Mark Lohman, Design: Ramirez Design, Inc.

p. 136: (top) Photo © Mark Lohman, Design: Ramirez Design, Inc.; (bottom) Photo © Brian Vanden Brink, Design: Robinson + Grisaru Architecture

p. 137: Photo © Jennifer Cheung and Steven Nilsson, Design: Heather Lenkin of www.lenkindesign.com

p. 138: (left) Photo © Jack Coyier Photography, Design: Ania Lejman, www.aldco.com; (right) Photo © Jack Coyier Photography

p. 139: (left) Photo © Jennifer Cheung and Steven Nilsson, Design: Heather Lenkin of www.lenkindesign.com; (right) Photo © Mark Lohman

p. 140: Photo © Jennifer Cheung and Steven Nilsson, Design: Heather Lenkin of www.lenkindesign.com

p. 141: Photos © Jennifer Cheung and Steven Nilsson, Design: Heather Lenkin of www.lenkindesign.com

pp. 142–143: Photo © Jennifer Cheung and Steven Nilsson, Design: Heather Lenkin of www.lenkindesign.com

CHAPTER 4

p. 144: Photo © Mark Lohman

p. 145: (top to bottom) Photo © Mark Lohman, Design: Ramirez Designs Inc.; Courtesy of Fermob; Photo © Jack Coyier, Design: John Bilac, Picture Perfect Construction (installation), www.pictureperfectconstruction.com; Photo © Mark Lohman, Design: Rhino Sports/Dream Courts

p. 146: Photo © Jennifer Cheung and Steven Nilsson, Design: Heather Lenkin of www.lenkindesign.com

p. 147: Photos © Jack Coyier Photography, Design: Gary Mason, Sanctuary Landscape Design

p. 148: (top) Photos © Jack Coyier Photography, Design: Jon Goldstein of Jonny Appleseed Landscape, Inc., www.jonnyappleseed.net; (bottom) Photo © Jack Coyier Photography, Design: Katie Moss Landscape Design, www.katiemoss.com

p. 149: Photo © Jack Coyier Photography, Design: Jon Goldstein of Jonny Appleseed Landscape, Inc., www.jonnyappleseed.net

p. 150: Photo © Jennifer Cheung and Steven Nilsson, Design: Heather Lenkin of www.lenkindesign.com

p. 151: (top) Photo © Mark Lohman, Design: Tom Stout Landscape Design and Abramson Teiger Architects; (bottom left) Photo © Mark Lohman, Design: Maraya Droney Design, Marlene Ayerle, and Brian Lehrman; (bottom right) Photo © Mark Lohman, Design: Burdge & Assoc.

p. 152: (top) Photo © Jack Coyier Photography, Design: ARTECHO Architecture and Landscape Architecture/Pamela Palmer, www.artecho.com (bottom) Photo © Mark Lohman, Design: Atlas Design and Ray Kinner Builders

p. 153: (top) Photo © Mark Lohman, Design: Ramirez Design Inc.;

p. 154: (1) Photo © Brian Vanden Brink, Design: Elliott Elliott Norelius Architecture; (2) Photo © Jennifer Cheung and Steven Nilsson, Design: Carolyn Watson; (3) Photo © Jack Coyier Photography, Design: John Bilac, Picture Perfect Construction (installation), www.pictureperfectconstruction.com

p. 155: (top) Photo © Jennifer Cheung and Steven Nilsson; (bottom) Photo © Mark Lohman, Design: Houston/Tyner Architects, Brad Jenson Construction, and Kathryne Designs

p. 156: Photo © Mark Lohman

p. 157: (left) Courtesy of Maku Furnishings; (right) Courtesy of Fermob

p. 158: (left) Courtesy of Sunbrella fabrics; (right) Photo © Mark Lohman, Design: Ramirez Design Inc.

p. 159: Photo © Jack Coyier Photography, Design: Katie Moss Landscape Design, www.katiemoss.com

p. 160: Photo © Jennifer Cheung and Steven Nilsson, Design: Heather Lenkin of www.lenkindesign.com

p. 161: (top) Photo © Jack Coyier Photography, Design: Katie Moss Landscape Design, www.katiemoss.com; (bottom) Photo © Mark Lohman, Design: Atlas Design and Ray Kinner Builders

p. 162: Photos © Jack Coyier Photography, Design: Wendy Harper, www.wendyharper.com

p. 163: Photo © Jack Coyier Photography, Design: ARTECHO Architecture and Landscape Architecture/Pamela Palmer, www.artecho.com

p. 164: (top) Photo © Mark Lohman, Design: Maraya Droney Design, Marlene Ayerle, and Brian Lehrman; (bottom) Photo © Jack Coyier Photography, Design: Katie Moss Landscape Design, www.katiemoss.com

p. 165: Photo © Jack Coyier Photography, Design: ARTECHO Architecture and Landscape Architecture/Pamela Palmer, www.artecho.com

p. 166: Photo © Mark Lohman Design: Houston/Tyner Architects, Brad Jenson Construction, and Kathryne Designs

p. 167: (top) Photo © Jack Coyier Photography, Design: Jon Goldstein of Jonny Appleseed Landscape, Inc., www.jonnyappleseed.net; (bottom) Mark Lohman Design: Burdge & Assoc.

p. 168: Photo © Jack Coyier Photography, Design: John Bilac, Picture Perfect Construction (installation), www.pictureperfectconstruction.com

p. 169: Photos © Jennifer Cheung and Steven Nilsson Design: Carolyn Watson

p. 170: Photo © Jennifer Cheung and Steven Nilsson, Design: Heather Lenkin of www.lenkindesign.com

p. 171: (top) Photo © Jennifer Cheung and Steven Nilsson ; (bottom) Photo © Mark Lohman, Design: Richard Turner Architect

p. 172: (left) Photo © Philip Beaurline; (right) Photo © Mark Lohman, Design: Tom Stout Landscape Design and Abramson Teiger Architects

p. 173: Photo © Brian Vanden Brink, Design: Hutker Architects

p. 174: Photo © Mark Lohman, Design: Ramirez Design Inc.

p. 175: Photo © Mark Lohman, Design: Ramirez Design Inc.

p. 176: Photos © Mark Lohman, Design: Rhino Sports/Dream Courts

p. 177: (top) Photo © Jack Coyier Photography, Design: Jon Goldstein of Jonny Appleseed Landscape, Inc., www.jonnyappleseed.net (bottom) Photo © Mark Lohman,

Design: Rhino Sports/Dream Courts

p. 178: Photo © Jack Coyier Photography, Design: John Bilac, Picture Perfect Construction (installation), www.pictureperfectconstruction.com

p. 179: (top) Photo © Jack Coyier Photography, Design: John Bilac, Picture Perfect Construction (installation), www.pictureperfectconstruction.com (bottom left) Photo © Mark Lohman, Design: Rhino Sports/Dream Courts (bottom right) Photo © Jennifer Cheung and Steven Nilsson

p. 180: Photo © Jack Coyier Photography, Design: Katie Moss Landscape Design, www.katiemoss.com

p. 181: Photos © Mark Lohman, Design: Burdge & Assoc.

p. 182: (top) Photo © Mark Lohman, Design: Ramirez Design Inc. ; (bottom) Photo © Mark Lohman

p. 183: (top) Photo © Mark Lohman, Design: Burdge & Assoc.; (bottom) Photo © Jack Coyier Photography, Design: Jon Goldstein of Jonny Appleseed Landscape, Inc., www.jonnyappleseed.net

p. 184: Photo © Jennifer Cheung and Steven Nilsson, Design: Carolyn Watson

p. 185: (top) Photo © Mark Lohman, Design: Barbara Butler Artist/Builder Inc. (bottom) Photo © Brian Vanden Brink

p. 186: (top) Photo © Mark Lohman, Design: Barbara Butler Artist/Builder Inc. ; (bottom) Photo © Mark Lohman, Design: Tom Stout Landscape

p. 187: Photo © Mark Lohman, Design: Burdge & Assoc.

p. 188: (top) Photo © Mark Lohman, Design: Barbara Butler Artist/Builder Inc. (bottom) Photo © Mark Lohman Design: Rhino Sports/Dream Courts

p. 189: Photo © Mark Lohman, Design: Barbara Butler Artist/Builder Inc.

CHAPTER 5

p. 190: Photo © Philip Beaurline

p. 191: (top to bottom) Courtesy Smith and Hawken; Photo © Jack Coyier Photography, Design: ARTECHO Architecture and Landscape Architecture/Pamela Palmer, www.artecho.com; Photo © Jack Coyier Photography, Design: Ania Lejman, www.aldco.com; Photo © Philip Beaurline

p. 192: Photo © Jack Coyier Photography, Design: Gary Mason, Sanctuary Landscape Design

p. 193: (top) Photo © Mark Lohman, Design: Volante Design; (bottom) Courtesy of Metro Shed

p. 194: Photo © Jack Coyier Photography, Design: Ania Lejman, www.aldco.com

p. 195: Photos © Mark Lohman, Design: Atlas Design and Ray Kinner Builders

p. 196: (top) Courtesy of Modern Sheds; (bottom) Photo © Mark Lohman, Design: Don & Jackie McCune Design, Inc.

p. 197: Photo © Mali Azima, Design: Southeastern Construction

p. 198: Photo © Mark Lohman, Design: Houston/Tyner Architects, Brad Jenson Construction, and Kathryne Designs

p. 199: (top) Photo © Brian Vanden Brink, Design: Sam Williamson, Landscape Architect; (bottom) Photo © Mark Lohman

p. 200: Photo © Jennifer Cheung and Steven Nilsson

p. 201: Photo © Mark Lohman, Design: Tom Stout Landscape Design and Abramson Teiger Architects

p. 202: (top) Photo © Jack Coyier Photography, Design: ARTECHO Architecture and Landscape Architecture/Pamela Palmer, www.artecho.com; (bottom) Photo © Philip Beaurline

p. 203: Photo © Jack Coyier Photography, Design: ARTECHO Architecture and Landscape Architecture/Pamela Palmer, www.artecho.com

p. 204: (left) Courtesy of Tumbleweed; (right) Photo © Philip Beaurline

p. 205: Photo © Philip Beaurline, Design: Andy Andrews; SLDC Architects, Ltd.

p. 206: Photo © Jack Coyier Photography, Design: Katie Moss Landscape Design, www.katiemoss.com

p. 207: (top) Photo © Jack Coyier Photography, Design: Katie Moss Landscape Design, www.katiemoss.com; (bottom) Courtesy of Metro Shed

p. 208: (top) Courtesy of Modern Sheds; (bottom) Photo © Philip Beaurline

p. 209: Photo © Mark Lohman

p. 210: (left) Photo © Philip Beaurline; (right) Photo © Eric Roth

p. 211: Courtesy of Walpole Woodworkers

p. 212: (1) Courtesy of Private Garden; (2) Photo © Philip Beaurline, Design: Daggett & Grigg Architects

p. 213: (3) Photo © Mark Lohman; (4) Photo © Mark Lohman; (5) Courtesy of Private Garden; (6) Courtesy of Private Garden

p. 214: (1) Courtesy of Private Garden; (2) Photo © Jennifer Cheung and Steven Nilsson

p. 215: (3) Photo © Jennifer Cheung and Steven Nilsson; (4) Photo © Jennifer Cheung and Steven Nilsson